Sing It Pretty

MUSIC IN AMERICAN LIFE

*A list of books in the series appears
at the end of this book.*

Sing It Pretty

A MEMOIR

Bess Lomax Hawes

University of Illinois Press
Urbana and Chicago

Library of Congress Cataloging-in-Publication Data
Hawes, Bess Lomax, 1921–
Sing it pretty : a memoir / Bess Lomax Hawes.
p.   cm. — (Music in American life)
Includes index.
ISBN-13 978–0–252–03313–1 (cloth : alk. paper)
ISBN-10 0–252–03313–2 (cloth : alk. paper)
ISBN-13 978–0–252–07509–4 (pbk. : alk. paper)
ISBN-10 0–252–07509–9 (pbk. : alk. paper)
1. Hawes, Bess Lomax, 1921– 2. Folklorists—United States—
Biography. 3. Arts administrators—United States—Biography.
I. Title.
GR55.H39A3   2008
782.42162'130092—dc22 [B]   2007030924

For Corey, Naomi, Nick,
and the grands

Contents

Photographs follow pages 60 and 102.

Acknowledgments

The quotation in chapter 5 from Woody Guthrie is © copyright 2007 by Woody Guthrie Publications, Inc. All rights reserved. Used by permission.

The quotation in chapter 6 from "The Train That Never Returned" by Pete Seeger is © copyright 2007 by Pete Seeger. All rights reserved. Used by permission.

A portion of chapter 7 is abridged from "Yeast to Make the Bread Rise," a keynote address presented by Bess Lomax Hawes at the Children's Music Network National Gathering, Petaluma, California, October 15–17, 1999.

A portion of chapter 8 is abridged from "Some Observations on the Law and Order of the Playground," by Bess Lomax Hawes, chapter 2 in Eli M. Bower and Lloyd Shears, *Games in Education and Development* (Springfield, Ill.: Charles C. Thomas Publications, 1974). Courtesy of Charles C. Thomas Publisher, Ltd., Springfield, Illinois.

A greatly abridged version of "Happy Birthday to You," submitted as an M.A. thesis by Bess Lomax Hawes to the University of California, Berkeley, in 1970, appears in chapter 9.

The excerpt in chapter 14 from Lincoln Caplan's "Pass It On," which appeared in the Talk of the Town column in the *New Yorker,* October 1, 1984, is used with permission of the author.

A portion of chapter 15 appeared in an earlier form in the introduction to *American Folk Masters: The National Heritage Fellowships,* by Steve Siporin (New York: Harry M. Abrams, 1992). It appears here with permission of the publisher.

Sing It Pretty

Bess Lomax Hawes was born in January 1921 at Austin, Texas, the fourth and last child of the noted American folksong collector John Avery Lomax and Bess Bauman Brown.

ONE

Getting Started

When I was a little girl my family lived in East Texas out in the country, and so my mother decided to teach me at home. She had already taught me to read—and before me, my big sister and two older brothers—for she loved to teach. And she always said she was going to take her last child, Bess, as far as she could, for she was also a great lover of learning.

So until I was ten years old I stayed home with Mother, and she taught me Latin and piano and medieval history and lots of unusual things. But she also taught me the day-to-day things. She taught me how to sew, for example. I remember sitting on the floor with her ragbag, which was full of scraps of material from all the clothes Mother had made for us, and sort of folding doll clothes out of them.

But then I had to learn how to do it right. My mother was a great believer in doing things right. So she gave me a Latin motto to think about every day. She gave all her children different Latin mottoes. My brother Alan's was *Festina lente*, which means "Make haste slowly." Mine, though, was *Faciendo ediscere facere*, which means "By doing, you learn to do." She would tell me over and over, "By reading, you learn to read, Bess," "By running, you learn to run," and "By sewing, you learn to sew."

So I learned how to work her old foot-treadle Singer sewing machine. She would give me the front page of the *Dallas Morning News*, and every morning, with the machine unthreaded, I had to sew up and down the news-print columns and around the photographs until I learned just how to sew a straight line and turn a neat corner. And then I had to learn how to embroi-der, because that was what all little girls did in my part of the country—at least little Anglo girls like me. All of my friends knew how to do the French knot and the outline stitch, and the lazy daisy and the featherstitch too.

Every November, my mother and I would go to the dime store and I would get to pick out the presents I was going to make for Christmas. In those days you could buy dresser scarves or table napkins or pillowcases that had designs stenciled on them with blue dots, and "embroidering" was to cover those blue dots with French knots and lazy daisies in different colors, so it would turn out to be a special present that you yourself had made. So, after I had picked out the item I wanted to embroider for my sister or my grandmother, I would go to the embroidery thread counter and pick out the colors. There was always white embroidery thread, I remember, and lots of pastels—pale green, pink, lavender, yellow, light blue—and sometimes black, and sometimes red and orange. I agonized. One year, I remember coming home with red and black and green and pink and lavender and white. My big sister said, "Honey, you don't want to use that red and black. They won't blend. You want it to blend and be pretty." I thought it might be pretty, but I tried it and it wasn't. It didn't blend, and I had to pick it all out and start all over again.

I loved to sit on the ragbag like a beanbag chair. In the bag were scraps from my dresses and the other children's blouses and Father's old business shirts. Those pieces of cloth weren't scarlet or magenta or orange, they were lavender and aquamarine and pale blue. And they were solid colors or small prints, reflecting the conservative family we actually were (or thought we were).

Every once in a while my mother would load the ragbag into the car and we would go to see the quilt lady, who lived about two miles away. This was during the Depression and everybody did what they knew how to do to make a few cents, and this lady really knew how to make quilts. Mother and she would look over all our scraps, and she would get out all the pat-terns she had cut out of newspapers, and they would decide which patterns would look best with the material at hand. The idea was not to have to buy any extra cloth, if possible; times were too hard to spend a penny you didn't have to spend. But this lady could take all our old bits and pieces and make absolutely beautiful quilts out of them. Mother always said she was a real artist at her work.

So all the quilts on our beds turned out to be blendy. They were made out of the clothes we wore and the colors we had chosen and the aesthetic principles we had learned: neat corners, straight lines, balanced curves, precise workmanship, unemphasized dividing lines, subtle color gradations. It's actually a wonderful system; around the world it has produced some beautiful effects, from Italian paintings to British flower gardens to Chinese porcelains to East Texas quilts. And it is still strong in me, in spite of the relatively short period of my life I was exposed to it. The last sewing project I have undertaken was for a new baby in the family and I laugh sometimes when I look at it; for with a world of color and gaiety to choose from, I picked out white and pale green and the sweetest pale yellow, because I thought they would work up together just so pretty.

But there are many other enduring, striking, and productive color palettes besides the one my family favored. American Indians in their traditional work often emphasize clear primary colors, each of which may represent a different direction: east, north, south, west, up, down. They point a way and make distinctions between elements rather than shading things together. Many African American quilters prefer to emphasize movement and energy through brilliant color-soaked contrasts that almost vibrate to the eye—magenta and lime green and sulfur yellow, and lots of black to set it all off. The colorful visual playfulness of many Mexican traditions depends on the use of shocking pink and scarlet and peacock blue, often all at the same time.

A few years ago a folklorist friend in Arizona told me that he had noticed that many of the hottest local piñata makers were turning out highly uncharacteristic white and pale pink and baby blue piñatas. They were still fanciful and charming, but where were the swirling combinations of lime green, electric blue, and brilliant reds? All of a sudden, Arizona piñata makers seemed to be turning to pastels in a truly major aesthetic change, and people became really curious as to what was going on. Was there a kind of intriguing art nouveau idea coming up north from Mexico? Maybe piñata makers were hoping by imitation to enter a possibly more lucrative market? Or had the art teachers with their color wheels gotten in there and persuaded the craftspeople to work for gentler, more melding effects, instead of looking across the color spectrum for brilliance and contrast? Such fundamentals as color choices don't generally change as rapidly as this one had.

The most likely cause of it all turned out to be embarrassingly simple. A fine Arizona folklorist named Jim Griffith turned up the vital information that, at that time, there was only one wholesale paper company servicing the whole state. Executives in this fortunate company had observed that the majority of tissue papers bought in bulk across the state were light colored. Gift and department stores used white, light blue, or pale pink tissues to wrap up their first-class merchandise, and it was to those stores that the big-quantity sales were made. The sales of burnt orange, emerald, crimson, aquamarine, and royal purple tissue papers were negligible by contrast. So a strictly business decision had been made. This not only confirms the immediate point—that art is often deeply affected by what materials are available—but another point that proved true throughout my life: the rich tend to get richer and the poor, poorer.

In this particular case, though, my friend Jim (a creative fellow himself) considered the situation for a while; and then, slowly, industrial-sized rolls of brilliant color-soaked tissue papers began to stockpile in his own private living room closet. And then it just somehow worked out that any piñata maker in southern Arizona could quietly take away, on a pay-as-you-go system, a yard (or a mile, as needed) of any of the colors, according to his own aesthetic taste. And by and by, things began to subside back to normal. A reasonable number of pastel or snow-white piñatas appeared in the stands along with an ample quantity of the old-fashioned brightly colored ones, and soon everyone had forgotten all about the great southern Arizona color change. Really it hadn't so much changed as it had cut a few capers. The availability of materials is so critical in artistic conception and production; and it is so often in the control of business, rather than aesthetic, entrepreneurs.

The happy thing about this story is that at least the largest part of the aesthetic authority had finally returned to the makers who, as my mother might have recognized, had grown up using their own formulation of *Faciendo ediscere facere:* by doing, you learn to do. For after all, they were the ones who knew how to make piñatas.

During the years I am writing about, roughly 1921–31, my family turned out to be pretty conservative in the area of music, although in a complicated sort of way. We displayed an impressive stand-up Victrola in our living room, and Mother bought the family a serious collection of RCA Victor

Red Seal albums of classical music—Beethoven, Chopin, Tchaikovsky, Bach (her favorite). For me, the album containing the entire score of Gilbert and Sullivan's *Mikado* was the best of all, and eventually I learned all of Nanki-Poo's solos by heart. He was the romantic tenor, but his sweetheart's soprano solos were too high for me and I couldn't sing along with her.

Most children in those days were encouraged by their parents, as well as their teachers, to memorize piano pieces, songs, poetry, speeches, declamations, Bible quotations—anything that might be presented for the edification and entertainment of family and, most especially, guests. Although our big Victrola was generally admired as top of the line and we all thought it sounded gorgeous, I do not ever recall a record having been put on it after dinner for the enjoyment of guests. It took our friends a long time to drive out to our "House in the Woods," and guests were too special and refreshing to allow a mere machine to take over the conversation.

Everybody wanted to talk themselves, and dinner often ended with an unannounced and sometimes prolonged battle of storytelling between Father and the guests' principal teller. Young folks sat at the table and laughed along with the grown-ups until we finally were excused and sent outside to play or do homework. Sometimes we had to say our "pieces" first, but we were never, ever, invited to participate in the storytelling. Dinner and after-dinner entertainment were grown-up affairs.

And even after the company went home, if it hadn't gotten too late, it was Father who would read to the assembled family. That was always an important event. After the table was cleared and the dishes washed (by various combinations of Mother and the children), we would all move into the living room and settle in our every-night places—me on the floor behind Father's big chair (with a coloring book in case I found myself too bored by the evening's selection), Mother in her rocking chair with some mending, the others scattered around the big room. Father did the choosing, and he galloped us through *A Tale of Two Cities, Huckleberry Finn, As You Like It, The Jungle Book, David Copperfield, Treasure Island*, a hilarious book of the times called *Pigs Is Pigs, Tales of Robin Hood*, some of O. Henry's short stories, *A Midsummer Night's Dream*, and most of the narrative poems in an enormous volume of classic English poetry.

Father read well. If he didn't like what he was reading he would throw the book aside in disgust, and he always teared up a bit on the sad parts and put plenty of power into the fight scenes. Looking back, I think he must have developed a major skill at skipping, a kind of graceful on-the-fly, imperceptible editing. We could not possibly have finished all the books that I remember, but I still remember them as wholes and their emotional impact continues strong. It was quite an education, but our parents were proud of their own education and proud to be feeding the classics into their children.

Both Father and Mother had themselves grown up in the era of the Chautauquas, and they attended those gala cultural events as often as they could. In later years they became strong supporters of adult education, as did many other people of the period, most of whom had needed to struggle hard for the little learning afforded them by the country schools available to most young people. So both my loving parents went to all the lectures, concerts, poetry recitals, and debates that became available to them from the great wide world of intellectual sophistication and culture. And their standards became very high and even a bit classy. They prided themselves, like lots of other Texans at the time, on being in the forefront of the arts. But they both attended singing schools, whenever they came along.

In those days an itinerant music teacher might get the word put around that Professor So-and-So would be organizing a singing school for six weeks on Tuesday evenings at the local school house, pay at the door. Father described the students as generally a pretty mixed bunch—men, women, children, locals, visitors, anyone who could afford the small lesson charges. Everybody had a great time, apparently. The professor taught them their do-re-mi's first, and then a bit of standard notation. But after all that discipline came the part everyone had really come for: the new and old songs from the songbooks that each teacher passed around for classroom use.

There were always the grand old hymns: "Shall We Gather by the River?" and "We Are Bound for the Promised Land"; some sociable songs: "Aunt Dinah's Quilting Party," "The Spanish Cavalier," "Sailing, Sailing over the Bounding Main"; a few songs for the children: "Polly Wolly Doodle All Day" or "Skip to My Lou"; and finally special songs for special performances. For instance, Father occasionally would solo for us in a great bass voice that he reserved for such comic turns as—

Father: BASSO PROFUNDO IS MY NAME
    MY VOICE IS VERY LOUD AND STRONG
    I SING THE NOTES AND SOME TUNES TOO
    AND SOMETIMES SING A SONG!
    I SING ALONE . . .

Male treble (usually my brother Alan, under protest, a teenager at
the time): Why sing alone?
Father: BECAUSE THERE'S NO ONE ELSE CAN SING ONE HALF AS WELL
AS I!
Male treble (really squeaking): Let me but try . . .
Father: WHAT, YOU? OH, HA HA HA HA HA!
WHAT, YOU? OH, HA HA HA HA HA!

The only times I can myself remember Father singing "Basso Profundo"
were actually in the car. We sang a lot in the car, mostly all together. We
had an old-time, four-door Ford then and getting a family of any size into
it was always a squeeze. Father sat in the front right seat and commented
on the state of the crops and the local political situation. Mother sat in the
left front seat and drove. Somehow she had also become responsible for the
car itself, seeing to its needs for gasoline and water and occasionally giving
it a grease job. For that she would spread a pad of newspaper on our gravel
driveway, drive the car into position over it, and then slide herself under it
on her back in her usual housedress and stockings, quite decorously. It was
one of those many things in our household that had to be done, and done
well.

Our car trips through central Texas were long, hot, and boring. We
drove no faster than twenty-five miles per hour, the scenery was not all
that exciting, and there was little we could do in the back seat except nap
or play games. Sometimes we made up games; my older sister Shirley once
complained bitterly to my mother that I (at about five) had spent an entire
trip blowing down the back of her neck and then yanking her skirt up so
that I could watch the goose bumps come out on her legs.

A more sociable, family-invented game—"Dog"—was a feature of every
trip. The rules were simple. Anyone seeing a dog out of the car window
would holler "Dog!" (rather like "Whale Ho!"), and the first to make the call
got a point. When we drove through small towns where the dog frequency
was high, things could get so exciting that even Mother and Father would
join in.

But most of the time when we were bored somebody would start up
a song. Anybody could start one. Others of the family joined in or they
did not; in the latter case the lead singer usually faded out in discomfort.
Father often was the best starter—he had a great swing and energy to his
singing.

Come along, boys, and listen to my tale
I'll tell you of my troubles on the old Chisholm Trail
    Come a ti yi youpi youpi yay, youpi yay
    Come a ti yi youpi youpi yay

I woke up one morning on the old Chisholm Trail
A rope by the hand and a cow by the tail
    Come a ti . . .

"The Old Chisholm Trail" could last a good half hour, for all of us knew verses to throw in when Father's memory flagged. He explained to us that an old-timey cowpuncher had once informed him that the song was as long as the trail between Abilene, Texas, and Kansas City, Missouri. When we finally made it to Kansas City or simply got bored, Father might well start up another of his favorites—"Doney Gal" or "Whoopie Ti Yi Yo, Get Along You Little Dogies." He was not trying to instruct us, he was not trying to teach us about the history of the cattle business; he was just singing some songs he knew that were good songs and fun to sing.

We all knew that Father had "collected" these songs when he was young and had published a book of them in 1910 titled *Cowboy Songs* with an introduction by then-president Theodore Roosevelt, but to us they were just songs that cowboys used to sing. I do not recall the term "folksong" ever having been used to identify such songs during those years. They were plain old songs, or cowboy or railroader or coal miner songs, or they could be identified by their purpose—love songs or hymns, for example—that tacitly claimed a slight change in our singing style. And we never had to learn them and we never were taught them. They were just one of the many ways of making music that our parents showed us so as to stretch our characters and learn a bit more about how the world operated and to have some fun.

We usually sang in unison, the same notes all together, although occasionally Father or my big brother John would give a deep bass run-in (so-la-ti-do) to carry us into the next verse of a lively hymn. Mother had a very good ear and was really the only one of the family who could harmonize reliably. Occasionally she would move into a self-composed alto part. One afternoon at home she taught me a sentimental song of the period, and when we finally sang it together and her warm alto filled in my young soprano, I thought it was the most beautiful music I had ever heard. I still remember that, and that I was as much a part of it as she was; we sort of melted together:

'Nita, Jua-nita, ask thy soul if we should part
'Nita, Jua-nita, lean thou on my heart

Meanwhile, back at the Dallas house, the upright living room piano and our impressive standing Victrola were rarely idle. In some mysterious family enclave, of which I was not a part, it had been decided that I should become a pianist. I thought that sounded nice, and anyway I was biddable and cooperative as usual. We started out with once-a-week lessons with an excellent local teacher who pleasantly and simultaneously enticed and bulldozed me into an advanced repertoire for an eight-nine-ten-year-old. I enjoyed it though, the family were all pleased to have harbored a possible wunderkind, and my mother spent every hour of my twice-a-day, two-hour-long practice periods sitting on the piano bench with me. She and Father also saw to it that I attended every major concert of the great solo virtuosos of the times. I didn't think of it in these terms then, but it is clear to me now that from Mother's point of view I was not just taking piano lessons, I was becoming a pianist.

My sister Shirley, the oldest of the four of us children (she was sixteen when I was born), must have been far harder for Mother to handle. She was the beauty of the family, vivacious, intelligent, charming, a perfect flapper, which she immediately became as soon as she could learn the style. She wore her skirts way up over her knees and sat in the family hammock in the back yard, played the ukulele, and flirted with the UT and SMU fellows who hung around constantly. And she sang all the daring songs of the day—"Five Foot Two, Eyes of Blue," "Show Me the Way to Go Home," "Bye-Bye Blackbird," and "When the Red, Red Robin Goes Bob-Bob-Bobbin' Along." To me, she epitomized glamour in her pale blue chiffon party dress studded with gold beads from Paris.

She also bought 78 rpm records for our decorous Victrola machine—the latest and hottest hits. During the late 1920s and early 30s the developing recording industry was trying to figure out which way (or ways) it could most profitably go. Classical music seemed to have been preempted by RCA Victor, but there was always dance music and semiclassical music; and then in various parts of the country there were other kinds of music that the folks in those places really seemed to like and would lay out hard cash for—polka music, fiddle music, different kinds of religious music, blues. Nobody seemed to know much about these strange products, but the recording companies decided during these open times to take a number of chances that they might never take later.

And so my jazzy sister Shirley bought and put on the family Victrola some of the early jazz recordings. I have to say Mother sometimes shuddered and her back went stiff when she heard them, but she clamped her mouth shut and never said a word, at least not in front of me. I don't remember them in any detail, except for a lady named Bessie Smith who sang a song about a flood on the Mississippi River. I know there were other of her recordings that we had, but this is the one I remember from my childhood, and it still sounds just the same. "Backwater Blues," she sang, and I think of it every time I hear of a devastating flood on the Ohio or on the Mississippi, or in Pakistan or Guatemala.

There were lots of other songs I heard on those early commercial records, names I never did remember, but I remember loving the thumpy cross-rhythmed banjos and the jazzy piano riffs. And I did find myself wondering sometimes about why all these folks seemed to like jelly roll so much. I had tasted jelly roll myself, although Mother was never strong on desserts; but she had occasionally taken me into the bakery, and I had discovered that there were lots of other fine cakes there that seemed to me just as delicious looking. It was another of the mysteries of adulthood yet to be solved.

When Mother died at the age of fifty in 1931 I was ten years old, and the memories I have described here stopped at that time. They would probably not have continued much longer anyway. The years from eight to ten are generally a kind of golden age when one is no longer a fractious, imperious baby and can begin to feel a bit synchronous with the world, chiming in with its rhythms and with one's place in it. Then the time comes along when one can't remain a child any more and must begin to take some personal responsibility, both for the infinitely complicated world and one's own uncontrollable and unpredictable self. I am sure that my life from eight to ten was not as innocent and joyful as I have described it, but it's nice to think that it could have been. And maybe it even was.

TWO

Growing Up

Though I didn't know it, by the age of ten I had had an excellent send-off into a new kind of life, especially the complex world of music. In the remote and largely rural Texas of that era, I had already heard a significant range of different styles and types of music, and I had learned that music is an occupation in which a person can achieve excellence and perhaps even earn a living. I had also discovered that the learning of music can be formal or informal or, mostly, both. But most of all, I had learned that I myself could do music—I could sing a little, and play a little, and listen to and enjoy and even understand some music. I felt confident, relaxed, and happy with music. And there was a whole world of organized sound yet to be heard. My problems turned out to be largely concerned with the extraordinary organization of people.

I will not now try to trace back all the things that happened to me during my adolescent years. But I will provide some vignettes of the most important events, which really means those that I have remembered most frequently and passionately.

After my mother's death, my poor grieving father—self-condemning and deprived all at one stroke of the major support structures of his own life—still had to take care of a ten-year-old girl who, I am sure, he loved very much. But he was alone in this very major responsibility.

He first sent me to the very finest school for the development of young ladies he could find. I had had no preparation for any such situation and all it entailed. Conflict was inevitable and wounding. I remember only going out to play hockey every day and never remembering which end of the field was "our" goal. I had never before seen a hockey stick or a hockey puck or a hockey goal for that matter, and I always hit the thing the wrong way and nobody wanted me on their side. I felt completely ignorant and totally clumsy (and so I was, in truth).

My misery was such that Father grabbed the first chance that came along to get me into another school, one where my cousin Virginia was teaching. It was on the wrong side of Dallas and full of children of Mexican or Mexican American ancestry. The first impression of this school I had was of a horrendous clanging and banging in every hall. I found out later that this scary noise was made by students closing their locker doors, but that made little difference, I was still confused and upset. Eventually I was given my own personal locker, but since I never could find it—or any of my classrooms either—I wandered around for weeks with a pair of imaginary hands over my ears and some real tears in my eyes. I never—ever—knew where I was. Somehow the incessant noisiness disoriented me.

My thoughtful and experienced cousin, Virginia Brown, then a teacher of elementary geography, called together a small group of fifth-grade Mexican American girls and gave them a special assignment: to see to it that I never got lost. She couldn't have made a better choice. All the children she appointed were automatically old hands at caring for the disabled, the simpleminded, the blind, the ill, the elderly, the infants—the long trail of the generally needful that poor people have to take care of themselves—and these ten- and eleven-year-olds looked me over and sized up my problems in an experienced, sympathetic, and almost professional manner.

Their first move was to force a short lunchtime on me, the time saved being devoted to teaching me how to catch a ball. My older brothers and sisters had occasionally thrown a ball in my general direction, but not like this. This was serious. I even learned some of the rudiments of baseball under their firm tutelage. Not one of them ever laughed at my clumsy efforts to run and throw and catch. And inside the school building, when that terrible bell would begin to clang and all the locker doors would start banging, there was always one of them beside my desk, ready to walk with me through the reverberating halls, getting me safely to my next class.

The following year, Father sent me off to Lubbock to live with my older sister and her baby and I never saw any of those little girls again. But I never did forget them. Years later when I was in high school in Austin, Texas, a vain, self-satisfied young teacher of Spanish emphasized in class that since he had been to Spain, he himself had a perfect Castilian accent. Therefore, he said, the local Spanish-speaking children of Mexican descent in the room should find another class, since they could never hope to understand anything he said.

Quite on my own I went to the principal's office to let him know about this outrage, totally confident he would agree with me that teachers shouldn't say such things to any class, let alone one with Mexican-born children in it. Before I could blink I found myself out in the hall, the principal having said only that my job was to learn Spanish, not to criticize teachers, and that he hoped with my distinguished background I was not trying to become a troublemaker.

That particular episode has informed my every reaction to the many human rights issues that have emerged during the years since. Father used to worry that I was being "radicalized" by my brother Alan and my peers in Bryn Mawr, where I undertook my major college studies. But I was already there.

For reinforcement, there was the Depression. Sometimes little things stay with you, and I remember one day running down the gravel driveway to the huge oak that marked the entrance to our house, so as to give Father a homecoming hug. Mother came too, and we all three walked back up to the house while he told us with horror what he had seen. "Every single car on every train I saw was black with the bodies of men riding on top or hanging from the sides. There are so many of them, the railroad police have stopped trying to get them off. God knows where they are going—just to the other end of the line, I guess, and they've got no idea if anything's going to be there for them. I just don't know what's happening to this country." That would have had to be in 1930 or 31, because my mother was still alive. And this was when I first heard anything about the Depression.

Eventually, Father gave up on the Dallas schools (and on learning how to braid my hair, since I couldn't do it myself) and it was then that he sent me out to Lubbock to stay with my older sister Shirley and her husband, Dr. Chris Mansell. Dr. Chris was a strong-muscled Texan football player/ intellectual with a gruff voice and an unexpectedly gentle touch. He and I eventually came to friendship because of his passion for European classical music, especially opera, an interest then shared by few in Lubbock except for the local Catholic priest. The three of us must have made quite a picture sitting in the living room listening to *Aida*.

My pretty, jazzy sister Shirley had turned into a pretty, jazzy mother and a popular Lubbock hostess. She still had her ukulele and we almost never stopped singing, mostly our favorite songs of the day: "Ain't She Sweet?" "It Had to Be You," "Melancholy Baby," "Sweet Child," "Has Anybody Seen My Gal?" "Just Me and My Shadow," and dozens of others. In between backyard barbecues (with singing) and well baby clinics, Shirley also organized and directed an active and interesting Girl Scout troop that I joined enthusiastically. My young Mexican friends in Dallas had trained me well: I could do most things other girls my age could do, and for the first time in my life I began to fit in with my peers. Every day seemed full of excitement and just plain fun.

But inside, I still felt I was different. And when my father married Ruby Terrill—a Latin scholar, the dean of women at the University of Texas, and a charming, twinkly, endlessly patient lady—I was taken to Austin where the two of them had already settled down. And there I started on another new way of living: much more serious, with much more attention given to scholastics. My greatest enjoyment was a crowd of interesting high school girls who could actually drive, and who drove very soberly their own cars— sort of teenage Girl Scouts. They had developed a marionette show about Peter Pan that we eventually took around to elementary schools. I got to do a lot of the singing for that show. But when I started into the University of Texas as a freshman at the age of fifteen, there was still no doubt in my mind that I was still an odd girl and still outside, really.

My intellectual and charismatic brother Alan, however, was also attending the University of Texas at that time, and he and his friends had an apartment I remember well—smoke filled and glamorous, where handsome young men would leap to their feet at especially fine points in the Beethoven symphony playing on the Victrola and pace the room, leading the orchestra with their graceful hands. In between, they would drink coffee and talk about political issues, and pacifism, and Marxism, and the rights of labor.

I drank it all in; it was so exciting and so new. These were active times on any university campus. There were peace committee booths on every sidewalk at the University of Texas, where I spent my first college year, and I eventually signed the peace pledge and promised never to assist in any kind of war for the rest of my life. I thought a lot about it ahead of time, and I took it very seriously (and still do, in many ways).

⌒

Poor Father, there were so many things changing all at once. He tried, with little assistance from his younger children, to cling to his earliest principles as one way for a seventy-year-old man to survive with dignity. But some of his favorite principles conflicted with others (as seems to happen often in the case of principles) and Alan and I took wicked delight in pointing that out to him. For instance, he wanted very much for me to become a "real" scholar (preferably in the classical languages, but possibly even in folklore), while he felt perfectly free to make fun of young women who were "all dried up" because "they can't get a husband because of their intellectual pretenses."

However, this was also the period in which he was doing a major part of his ultimate and perhaps his greatest fieldwork, coming home with Leadbelly as a house guest and introducing me to the Gant family, a wonderful family of singers who lived, at that time, in a six-room shanty beside the Trinity River. Each year the Trinity rose over its banks and flooded them out, and each year the Gants retreated with all their bits of belongings to the upper banks to wait for the river to go down. But that old river never could stop the flow of their extraordinary repertory of Anglo-American balladry and folksong.

Folkloring in those days was a family affair, and I learned early never to appear unoccupied for there was no end of work to do copying notes, song lyrics, and miles of correspondence on the typewriter. Father wrote all his letters and notes by hand with a dip pen in fine Spencerian script, and now Mother's focus on my becoming a competent typist paid off. I never regretted an instant of the boring and repetitive labor learning to type had cost me, for it was a grown-up and useful way to help, and everybody in our family was supposed to be a worker in those early years. I must have typed out hundreds of song lyrics, including a lengthy manuscript of bawdy songs someone had kindly lent Father. (I never knew whether he was aware of its contents before I handed in my typescript; at any rate, the subject never came up between us.)

This was also the period when Father began experimenting with making permanent field recordings. He had used an old cylinder machine to collect tunes for his first published song collection (*Cowboy Songs*) and had succeeded in getting the publisher to print about twenty of the hundred or so melodies he had recorded. The cylinders were made of wax and were very fragile—I remember Shirley telling me she had once found on the porch a box of old cylinders that had completely melted into a black puddle—but they only had to last long enough for Father to get them to a literate musician for transcribing (he couldn't read or write music himself). And for all of Father's talk of riding out to visit ranches with the recording machine "balanced on the pommel" of his saddle, it was neither portable nor easy to use. It had a big flaring horn like a morning glory that served as both microphone and speaker, and you had to stick your face down into the horn when you sang in order to get a good sound. Father found that quite a few of the cowboys he wanted to record didn't seem to share his enthusiasm for the new technology.

By the 1930s things had improved, of course, but only somewhat. The new machines were electric and they could cut pretty durable recordings on big acetate or aluminum discs, but they were still heavy, awkward, and finicky to use. There was nothing casual about using these machines or about making field recordings, but that suited Father, who wasn't at all casual about it himself. Father carefully worked out a program of songs for each person he recorded, selecting only the best songs from each singer's repertory. And his recording sessions were formal affairs. Each track on each disc would begin with an announcement: "This song is being recorded by Mr. So-and-So in such-and-such a town on the something day of August *for the benefit of the Library of Congress in Washington!*" He made it sound so important, as if the whole government was going to listen to each and every one of them. (And maybe, in a sense, that's just what did happen—things certainly aren't the same as they used to be.)

The recordings were made on heavy sixteen-inch discs. I used to have one of the old aluminum records around somewhere, but I never listened to it because the aluminum was so soft it needed to be played back using a cactus needle. In fact, one of my chores as a child was to grind cactus needles to shape. There was a little machine for this purpose, kind of like a pencil sharpener, and each time you played a record you had to grind the needle fresh (one of my many skills I've never been able to find a place for on my resume).

The recording machine the Library of Congress supplied for Father was an enormous thing weighing upwards of three hundred pounds and requiring a slew of full-size car batteries to make it go. I remember Father took the back seat out of our brand-new Ford and had a built-in platform made with special shock absorbers to carry the delicate burden. In spite of his best efforts, though, the machine broke down regularly, and it was as often back in Washington being repaired as it was out in the field being used.

It may well have been that unreliable and not-so-portable recording machine that led to the only formal fieldwork experience I remember with Father. We were traveling through Louisiana—I don't remember why, probably on a family trip to the Gulf Coast—when Father decided to stop off at the state prison at Angola to collect a particular song he had heard a convict sing on a previous visit. We didn't have the recording machine with us, so Father simply announced that morning that I would be going into the prison with him to write down the melody from a prisoner's singing. I don't know whatever gave him the idea that I could do this—I had never transcribed anything before. But Father's attitude was that this was just one more thing that needed to be done, and he was sure that I could do it. (Perhaps this was *his* version of *Faciendo ediscere facere*.)

I don't remember many details of that day, but I do remember that I dressed in my very best clothes—in those days properly raised southern girls dressed for any social occasion, even a visit to a prison. I was led into what must have been the visitors' room. There was a long panel of glass running down the center of the room, and there were a lot of prison people there, executives and guards and men with guns. The prisoner was led in and he sang the song to me enough times so I could learn it by heart, and then I wrote down what I had learned on some music paper I improvised. That was my procedure anyway, such as it was. I certainly didn't know what I was doing, but nobody else there knew how to do it either and it had to be done.

I have no idea what the poor prisoner made of it all. I expect he just figured he was getting in good with the prison administration by going along with this strange business. I don't even remember his name now, and I have no idea at all what happened to him. I certainly hope the whole episode did him some good, but how can I know?

The transcription I made never got published. A longer version of the same song from a Texas prison did eventually appear in one of Father's and Alan's books ("Godamighty Drag," *Our Singing Country*, pp. 398–99), but I'm afraid that my maiden effort in folksong collecting is no longer available. It may be moldering away in a box in an archive somewhere, or it may have been discarded long ago. But I still remember how the song went:

Vrs 3: June, Ju-ly, and Au-gust...

Oh Mama and Papa
    Whoa Lordy
Oh Mama and Papa
    God-a-mighty God knows
Done told me a lie, sir
    Oh Lordy
Done told me a lie, sir
    God-a-mighty God knows

Done told me they'd pardon me
    Whoa Lordy
Done told me they'd pardon me
    God-a-mighty God knows
Come next July, sir
    Oh Lordy
Come next July, sir
    God-a-mighty God knows

June, July, and August
    Whoa Lordy
June, July, and August
    God-a-mighty God knows
Done come and gone, sir
    Oh Lordy
Done come and gone, sir
    God-a-mighty God knows

It still is a memorable song (in a melancholy sort of way) and I am pleased to pass it along one more time.

Sometimes I get to thinking about all the songs I know—songs I've sung or just songs I've heard that got stuck in my head—and it kind of paralyzes me: do I know songs that *nobody* else in the world knows anymore? And if I do, what ought I to be doing about them?

By now, though, I expect I've either sung or taught almost every song I know to somebody somewhere at some time or other. Maybe they learned them, maybe they didn't—I don't know. It's a sort of cultural accident which songs stick and which songs don't. You just have to have faith: good songs survive.

THREE

Our Singing Country

The years following my mother's death were difficult for both Father and me. I was struggling with my deep anger over having been torn from my happy life in Lubbock, with my growing affection (possibly disloyal?) for my new stepmother, whom we called Deanie, with my increasing understanding of what Father was doing and how interesting it was, and with the whole implacable panoply of ever-threatening adolescent issues: What did I want to do with myself? What could I be any good at? There were just so many ways to go.

Father was doing for me—counter to what I may have felt at the time—the best that he could, and possibly more than could have then been expected of him. Eventually he resorted to what he had done with his two sons before: he put me to work on one of his new projects, in this case the editing of a new book on American folksong based on the fieldwork he and Alan had done during the previous years, mostly in the southern states. The finishing work would be undertaken at the Library of Congress.

I was just fifteen, and as Father, Deanie, and I drove together through Appalachia on our way from Texas to Washington, D.C., I really saw poverty for the first time in my life. I saw it in the skinny children who came out of the hills to swarm over Father's Ford sedan. And I heard it in the thin, hungering, lonesome voices of the women who sang for Father when he stopped to visit.

> You got to walk that lonesome valley
> You got to walk it by yourself
> Ain't nobody here can walk it for you
> You got to walk that lonesome valley by yourself

For me that became the theme song of the trip. I sang it constantly and with such melancholy conviction that Deanie was finally forced to suggest to me that, although she and Father enjoyed my backseat singing, it would be nice to hear something slightly more cheerful just every once in a while.

But in spite of the teenage dramatics I was strongly moved by what I saw, and later in Washington, when my brother urged me to attend the proceedings of the Senate's La Follette Committee investigation of poverty in the United States, I took up his suggestion. After that I never looked back, even though other powerful issues such as pacifism, ethnicity, and labor rights came along. To me they all seemed to flow from the primary problem of economic inequity and its interaction with the political system. And I still think so.

In Washington, I lived a new life style. Father, Deanie, and I occupied a small apartment on Capitol Hill, close enough to the Library of Congress that we could walk to work. I had worked at home for Father before, primarily typing his correspondence, but that was simple: I just copied someone else's words. Now I was helping bring something that hadn't existed before into the world; now what I was doing had genuine presence and importance. It could possibly even survive.

My major assignment was to search out other printed versions of every song that might be included in the new songbook (eventually titled *Our Singing Country*) in order to present Father and Alan with scholarly information for use in headnotes and editorial comments. One morning, Alan took ten minutes to give me a copy of each song under consideration, scribbling on each the appropriate names from the classic printed collections I should tackle first: Sharp, Belden, Child, Brown, Odum, Korson, Flanders, Jackson, et al. I had never before opened, nor indeed heard of, any of these volumes.

But I was young and energetic and ready to go, and although now it seems to me I was totally unqualified for such a responsibility, at the time

I just went to work. It turned out, among other advantages, to have been a very good way for me to learn the essential repertory of American folksong. And I turned out to be reasonably good at it too, although nobody ever told me I was or wasn't—I was just a worker on the project. I hauled mountains of books from the stacks to our working area, and I read, and read, and read. (*Faciendo ediscere facere* all over again, although I didn't think of it at the time.)

And when I wasn't reading I was listening, for Alan and I spent hours every day playing back every single song loudly, cataloging each one, transcribing the words, and locating any available field notes. Eventually the patience of our scholarly research neighbors was exhausted, and we were exiled to a small attic at the very top of the Library of Congress with only the pigeons for company. As we listened to hour after hour of field recordings day after day, the dust and the heat blew in as they had perhaps on the singers themselves, and the painted friezes and the gilded decorative panels filtered the roaring ax-chopping songs and the crashing shape note hymns down through the ornate and orderly library stacks below us. In the evenings, string quartets would play Schubert and Chopin in the ground-floor concert hall, but in the attics the unsilenced and unquenchable voices of southern working people sang on.

I loved it. Earphones were new enough to be glamour items for us, so we played everything in real-life volume the way we felt it was intended to be heard. And we played phrases or verses over and over, sometimes twenty or thirty times, until we were sure we understood exactly what was being sung—and in between, we argued about it. Even the pigeons abandoned us occasionally.

Once or twice a week, after supper, we would be joined by Father and Ruth Crawford Seeger, the music editor, and her husband, Charles Seeger, the musicologist, to review what we had done. These were important listening sessions during which the entire coverage, the editorial thrust, the audience, the overall style and content of the book were being hammered out. I tended then to think each discussion was about whether or not an individual song should be included, but in truth it was much, much more. We were gradually working out a series of philosophical compromises between Father, Alan, Ruth, and Charley (as I disrespectfully called the eminent Dr. Seeger).

Whose criteria of organization should be followed: the people primarily interested in the music, the people primarily interested in the poetry, or the singers themselves? Was it as important to reproduce as nearly as possible the exact notes of a singer's melody as to reproduce as exactly as possible the words sung? What about the use of dialect transcription? Which audience was most important: was it the general reader, the musical specialist, the academic specialist, the community song leader, the church choral director? There were so many of these questions it became obvious that they could never all be answered; but then they *had* to be answered in order to get anything done at all. What was going on, I suspect, was a general testing between coworkers, making sure that there were no solid principles and/or prejudices that everyone could not work with, no really serious boulders in the path.

It wasn't a simple debate. Father and Alan had some brush clearing to do, mostly on the conflict between their general political philosophies (which never were as far apart as they thought they were). Eventually, Father drew back in favor of Alan's editorship, in part due to his own declining energies as well as his desire to let Alan try it for himself and see how complicated it was. Father then took on the role of commander in chief, and although he didn't insist on being part of every decision so long as the book was publishable and reasonably timely, he did come roaring in to occasional meetings with enough vivacity and seniority to keep everyone in line.

Ruth and Charley were both almost completely new to the complexities of American traditional music, and they had a tendency to "mirate" (one of Father's words) over the exotica of the free-rhythm "hollers" and the delicate melodic tracery of some of the British ballad tunes. But they really did appreciate and value the great performances they heard; they had long listened to African and Asian music of as many kinds as they could get hold of, so they were ready to make the most sophisticated decisions. As time went on and the basic bookmaking battles had been fought, Charley gradually withdrew, leaving Ruth matched with and against Alan. And I was a child among them, taking notes. I wish I had been more thorough.

I remember only one occasion on which I ventured to express my own individual opinion. I told Alan one afternoon in the Library of Congress that I thought the book was including so many unusual songs that it was leaving out the ordinary, day-to-day songs that more people could enjoy. He asked me to give him an example, and I said, "Well, how about 'Goodbye, Little Bonnie, Good-bye'? You and Father recorded it just like you did 'Ain't Going Down to the Well No More.' There's more like that." Alan said something about how I had a right to get my own in sometime, and

I forgot all about it—until the book came out and there was "Good-bye, Little Bonnie, Good-bye."

And it just wasn't that good of a song. I have felt very slightly embarrassed about it until this day. My point had been reasonable and maybe important, but I had given an example that was only pleasant and certainly not outstanding. There's simply something about quality that is vital, no matter what you're dealing with, and you mustn't ever be shy about saying so. That's what I learned then; and it is still a difficult lesson for me, since the debate between the good/everyday and the exceptional/infrequent is chronic, and probably eternal, depending on who is doing the final editing. But in these times, I fear more decisions are going toward the day-to-day than to the exceptional, and among all my worries, this one stands unresolved.

Meanwhile my everyday social contacts were expanding almost daily—from traffic policemen to bibliographers to coffeehouse waitresses to library stacks workers. I had never had that kind of day-to-day meeting outside the family before. One day Father took me over to the Capitol and introduced me to the Texas congressmen, including the celebrated Senator Tom Connally ("the old likker-swigging reprobate," as Father used to call him affectionately), who patted me on the head and astonishingly pronounced me an addition to Washington social life. Then I got to know Harold Spivacke of the Library of Congress Music Division. But I was still awfully shy. I got perhaps best acquainted with the Seeger family—or some parts of it, for the Seeger family was just as complex and scattered as my own.

Charley was the patriarch of the Seegers, as my father was of the Lomaxes. I was often at the Seeger house when Charley came in from work in his Washington office, and I saw all the children and Ruth hastily reorganizing, clearing up the living room, putting the last touches on supper, and greeting him with hoorays and hugs. When I was seeing the Seegers often, it was mostly the second family—Ruth's and Charley's children: Michael, Peggy, Barbara, and the baby, Penny—who were at home. The older bunch (Charles Jr., John, and Peter) came home somewhat sporadically, but they had their own ritual greeting, as I discovered one Christmas: all those four, lean, over-six-foot men, including Charley himself, knelt down grumpily in a square and stood on their heads. It was quite a spectacle. I don't believe it was a nightly event, just when all four were together, which didn't happen all that often. But Charley was an early adherent of yoga and kept it up throughout his life. I would occasionally run into him in the back corridor of an international musicological meeting standing placidly on his head and cheerfully greeting friends passing by.

But for me during this period (the summer and autumn of 1937) it was Ruth who was my lodestone and guide. She was totally remarkable—a serious classical musician, pianist, and composer in her own right, married to an eminent music scholar who joined her in her passion to be surrounded by great music and great children. But she was the one who took care of them all and ran the whole house, with little help and little money, and kept on trying to be a totally involved musician. So she took on the job of working on *Our Singing Country* in her nonexistent spare time, and we all benefited from her incredible hard work. And then one day Father announced that the project needed a go-between and I was to be it.

I think Ruth herself was delighted at the idea; and I was delighted too, because as messenger girl I would be going on the bus several times a week back and forth between Ruth in Maryland and Father and Alan in Washington, carrying bits of manuscript, alternate music transcriptions, copies of the original discs, critiques, and messages both passionate and hilarious. It never occurred to anybody to hire a messenger (where would we have gotten the money?). Telephone calls to Maryland were expensive in those days, and I was right there and thrilled at the prospect, for I could do something exciting by myself and still observe at first hand the work of a professional of Ruth's caliber.

I marveled at her strategies. She took over only a little corner of a downstairs room and assembled a recording machine, a rack for the discs, a tiny desk, and a professional architect's drafting board on which she eventually copied her completed musical transcriptions in a gorgeous kind of penmanship that could have gone straight to the printer. She used pots of the blackest India ink and large thick sheets of the whitest music manuscript paper, and her calligraphy was superb, so that every day there was a new piece of beauty on the drafting board. Her minuscule desk contained pencils, note paper, and separate sheets on which she made a tick mark every time she listened to each song she transcribed—eighty or ninety times, some of them.

She used earphones, and no child or adult would consider interrupting her when she had them over her ears. She and my mother both had the same fearsome rule: there was to be absolutely no talking while music was being played, because it was disrespectful and rude. I still feel that way, and Peggy Seeger has told me she does too. It's an awfully demanding requirement sometimes.

When Ruth was working, she hardly seemed there at all. I remember one month when all the children came down with whooping cough, one after another. For many weeks, Ruth and I would be sitting together discussing the materials I had brought and we would hear a long drawn-out whoop and somebody's rush to the bathroom. Ruth would quietly take off her earphones, run upstairs to deliver a damp washcloth to the sufferer, and then come back downstairs to the kitchen to make a sustaining snack for the invalid (she worried a lot about their nutrition). But within ten minutes she and I would be back deep in discussion of some particular musical point she didn't think Alan had understood properly.

She was always listening. She used the recording disc for what she believed it to be—a true record of the music as played or sung, taking as her basic assumption that the music was sounding the way the player wanted it to sound, not in a failed imitation of something else. This was a remarkably sophisticated position, for most people at the time thought of the folksong as simple, natural, naive, spontaneous, self-generated, and definitely crude. A lot of people still do, really, and still believe in their heart of hearts that any Appalachian balladeer would gladly sing like an opera star, if the poor thing could only get the proper training.

Ruth's splendid classical education and democratic personality left her devoid of such snobbishness. She stoutly believed that her job was simply to move the music as performed into another form of communication—print—thereby allowing it to circulate in a different way. Most people then doing that kind of work (musical transcription) were content with an approximation of what they thought they heard. Ruth never was. When she had to approximate, she grieved over it, and agonized, and changed it back and forth interminably, and finally wrote footnotes saying she was sorry and that it wasn't exactly what she had hoped for.

In the meantime my brother Alan was surpassing even Ruth's strong commitment to social needs, social justice, and the vital importance of the special messages that ordinary people send through their music. He perhaps had had greater experience in the twisting and cramping effects of translating sound into print, so in producing this new book he was determined to make up for the separation of musicians, music, and performance that so clearly occurred during most publication. He thought a great deal about how to present the songs in *Our Singing Country* within their special places and times, how to bring their unknown singers into prominence, and how to convey his respect for their poetry, their passion, their artistry. He grouped the songs in terms of their use and their place of singing, rather than according to literary criteria; he included the singers' own comments and parts of their life histories as the songs' introductory material; he tried in every way he could conceive of to rejoin the artist with the art. These were truly radical years in the United States, and both Ruth Crawford Seeger and Alan Lomax were conjoined in an attempt to change the basic assumptions that had underlain both the academic and popular attempts to understand American music. And if you are going to support the changing of things, you must observe the small changes especially carefully, for they will lead you directly into the large.

So they argued. They argued a lot. They argued almost all the time, with rage and humor and affection and real anger. Like all the good New Dealers and all the good left-wingers of that time, they argued exhaustively and with enthusiasm. To cite one example, a mammoth battle over the blues song "Go Down, You Old Red Rising Sun" went on for weeks, the point at issue being whether in the second line the singer had sung "you redder than rouge rising sun" or "you redder than ruby rising sun." Alan's position was that no blues singer he had ever heard could consider singing such an awkward and unpoetic line as "redder than rouge," and the missing syllable was just the result of an accidental voice break; while Ruth maintained that the only problem with that was that "redder than rouge" was what the singer had actually sung—and she had listened enough times to prove it.

Alan had talked with, broken bread with, told jokes with, and spoken about the world with hundreds of singers by then. Ruth had not had a comparable chance, and so they often arrived at different conclusions. They also represented different backgrounds, different fields of learning, in some ways different aesthetic systems, and they were also different human beings. But they were trying together to do something new and honest, groundbreaking and important; and as I watched them struggle, I began to absorb some of the subtleties of art and the complexities of change.

And I began to shudder at the thought of the thousands of such difficulties that must be faced in the reconstruction of any past reality. In every case, there are the facts somewhere about what actually happened, the unassailable on-the-record performance that Ruth held was the vital element, the almost holy data. And then there were the issues she couldn't really take into account, because they weren't immediately perceivable on the disc: the singer's age and background, the intensity of a particular historical tradition or moment, the customary ways of telling a story in a particular community—all the surrounding information that can be summarized as context, the things that Alan tended to insist were vital. Where should the weight fall? Which was more important? Could some amalgam of perspectives develop that would be an improvement? Well, they struggled and they sweated and, to my mind, they came up with a volume that was worth all the work—not a final solution, but a pretty darned good beginning. And I am sure that, whether they recognized it at the time or not, it was worth it to them.

For if you really dig into something, all that energy comes back into you and makes you just slightly different than before. I believe that my brother was enormously influenced by Ruth Crawford Seeger's firm and loving identification with the unassailable recording, the depth and capacity of the varying sounds of American traditional music. She in turn was deeply affected by my brother's ever-attentive focus on the uncharted and complex relations between aesthetics and life itself, especially the sophistication and depth of the transmitted message. To my mind, both Alan's Cantometrics research and Ruth's *Folksongs for Children* books stand as later, independent creations giving testimony to the impact of those two intellectuals on each other.

And for me, I think we are fortunate that they met, and at a time in our history when to be called truly "radical" was a glowing compliment, and at a time when there was a project worth their combined efforts.

FOUR

Europe and Bryn Mawr

Eventually *Our Singing Country* arrived at what proved to be a disappointing publication day. The reception was only moderate. Father and Alan were disconsolate. Perhaps it was the wrong book and perhaps for the wrong time. Ruth Seeger, whose initial, vastly oversized, intensely scholarly introduction had been rejected by Father, Alan, and the Macmillan editors as unsuitable for a book for the general public, felt triply rejected and extremely bitter. Reviewers seemed to overlook the extraordinary—now become routine—inclusion of Franco- and Hispanic-American traditional music, along with many another of the book's special features. Alan's notions of the importance of traditional biographies of traditional singers and instrumentalists somehow melted into the general fog that seemed to be graying over anything that was not concerned with the ever-increasing European and Asian crises.

But Father had long planned to take Deanie and me to Europe, painfully trying to make good on a promise he had long ago made to Mother, and so off the three of us went in February 1938, the book essentially done and past us. We were accompanied, to my delight, by my charming and decorative University of Texas roommate, Elizabeth Watkins. After a horrendous five days on the ocean liner *Queen Mary*—not her fault, terrible weather conditions—we arrived in Paris late one night. I awoke the next morning in my massively luxurious feather bed and went to the window to get my first glimpse of the fabled city of lights. And it was snowing! Snow was still a glamorous commodity to me, and these were those picture-book large, gentle flakes that whirled a bit before settling slowly to the ground. A kind of sweet piping was coming from the courtyard below.

I woke Elizabeth and when we looked out there was an old man standing there in a heavy coat and a winter hat playing us a good morning on some kind of wooden fife—the very first day we were in Paris! It was a lovely, simple tune, as easy and as inevitable as "Down in the Valley" or "Go Tell Aunt Nancy." I found the words later in a French schoolbook, and I still sing it:

Dessous ma fenêtre est un oiselet
Toute la nuit chante, chante son chanson . . .

We threw him all the French coins we had and all three of us waved and smiled at each other. It was the most truly romantic thing that had ever happened to me, absolutely perfect in every detail. I hope the coins added up to something—we didn't know what they were.

Actually, I didn't know all that much about anything on that trip. I had bought a second-hand guitar in New York before we left. I didn't know how to play the guitar but was confident I could make it go, and fortunately the previous owner had printed in ink the tuning E A D G B E under each string up at the neck. Using my piano background, I first figured out what you had to do to make every string sound one or another of the notes in the C major chord, then a G chord, and I was off and playing—a few songs only, but I thought it was pretty exciting. I carried that guitar in its old beat-up case throughout Europe and never regretted it for a second. It was a comfortable old thing and put up with all the extra items I managed to wedge in.

It kept on snowing in Paris, and after my thrilling morning even I began to wish for more clement weather, so we went next to Marseilles and Nice in the south of France. Since we were making the trip up as we went along, we had a Council of Trip somewhere during those beautiful sunny days, perhaps even in Monte Carlo, and tried to sketch out what we wanted to do next. Elizabeth and I had persuaded our parents (only somewhat cynically) that the only reason we had wanted to make the entire trip was to learn French, and we needed more time in Paris to pursue our educational goals. Deanie was especially interested in the classic sites of Italy—Rome and Florence and perhaps even Sicily. Father, on the other hand, seemed to want only to take care of his "females" and their luggage. Even then it was sad that Father had left himself out of the party, except as caretaker. But he had the checkbooks and the authority, and so Elizabeth and I took off into Paris and he and Deanie took off into the classical world.

We planned to rejoin as a foursome in Vienna, where we all arrived shortly after the *Anschluss* to find the city full of soldiers and almost bare of civilians. I had really no understanding whatever of what was actually going on. I had come to Europe to have a good time and to enjoy a proper young girl's tour, like those in the books, and I was not prepared to look beyond the whipped cream in the coffee in the sidewalk restaurants or the occasional flirtation with the hotel busboys.

But Vienna proved to be just too uncomfortable for all of us—for reasons I didn't exactly understand, although reality was beginning to penetrate—and we left as soon as we could arrange passage on a boat down the Rhine to Budapest. For me, this was to have been the highpoint of the trip, and it turned out that nothing could blunt the impact of the marvelous scenery we passed through. I even saw a genuine goose girl—just like in the fairy tales—with a long staff, herding her white charges along the riverbank.

Budapest was fascinating, and I felt almost immediately that there was no way I could begin to understand it. It was just too complicated, and it had an element of special differentness about it that I have run into in other parts of the world since. I liked it and would have given it a longer try, but Father and Deanie were not really comfortable there and we soon started our next plan. Elizabeth and I wanted very much to see Prague and Great Britain before we went home. Father had discovered that the spas of northern Italy and the Tyrol had been physically and emotionally beneficial. We agreed to separate once more and reunite in northern Italy to start our voyage home.

Elizabeth and I visited the Budapest Youth Hostel and asked them to reserve us a couple of hostel beds in Prague, since we would be arriving by train late at night. When we reached the given address about 12:30 A.M., we found it to be a large building in the center of Prague and definitely closed. A passing Czech policemen kindly helped us find a safe overnight hotel. On returning the next morning, we discovered that our Budapest host had apparently been a Nazi and had referred us to the Prague young people's Nazi headquarters. We were, however, welcomed there by two handsome, well-prepped, English-speaking young Nazis who offered themselves as escorts as long as we could stay. I was scared; Elizabeth was braver. Anyway, there didn't seem any way out of the situation but to go along. And, I admit, at the time it did seem like a real adventure.

We were settled into a room in the building, and then the four of us started out on the town. The two young men were a smooth-talking, charming pair who began squiring us to the beautiful architectural sights of the city while gently trying to "explain" the young Fascist movement to us. They were assiduous in their attentions, and I must say I began to feel pretty special. Actually, I was emotionally, socially, and intellectually quite unprepared for being taken around by such dazzling young men; but after a few days I began to feel a deep conviction that there was something basically wrong with this whole situation, and I decided I wanted out.

Elizabeth, much prettier and much more experienced in the dating game than I, thought I was being chicken and said she herself had never had so much fun. The last evening they took us to a genuine German beer garden, where we clashed our steins together and sang in on the choruses and polkaed just the way I had seen in the movies. And then my young Nazi (I am ashamed to have forgotten his name—the other, more handsome one had made a beeline for Elizabeth and her beautiful blue eyes as soon as he saw her, and from then on we were two fixed pairs) took my hand and turned it over and said, "You don't have a real woman's hand. Yours is soft and uncalloused; it has never done any hard work. A good German girl would be ashamed of such a hand."

Having been a Girl Scout and built a log cabin and worked in Father's gardens till I dropped, I did not take kindly to his remarks. We were rather stiff on the ride home, while I thought about his many unclear answers to my naive questions about German invasions of other countries and what would eventually happen in Czechoslovakia. A complicating factor was that I was still clinging to the fundamental philosophy I had developed in the fifth grade—it was a generally left-wing position, but no more specific than most left-wing positions at the time—and the young Nazis talked social justice and the equality of peoples and the rights of mankind just like everybody else I knew. It was only when I asked for specifics that I began to realize that those great words meant something quite different to them. Well, both of those young men are probably dead by now. I hope they did not do too much damage before they left us.

Elizabeth did not then join me in my discomfort. I went alone to Nuremberg, where Elizabeth was to meet me before we took off for the British Isles. I was deeply disturbed by Nuremberg, perhaps because for the first time on the trip I was completely by myself. I stayed in a hostel, where on my first evening I was washing with my shirt off in the bathroom when the hostel hostess came in, screamed, and dropped the linens she was carrying. She later sent an English speaker to my bunk to inform me that nudity of any body part whatever was not permitted at any time in the hostel. She would provide decent covering for those who required it. Later that evening, I watched a group of organized teenage female hikers come into the hostel, dripping with sweat, scarlet with sunburn, groaning as they let themselves down into their bunks. Several of them tried to reach me in my bunk. I didn't know what they wanted, and I knew no German, but I tried to be friendly, providing them with at least a hand squeeze. On other days, I watched public movies from which young girls and young women emerged in floods of tears, heaving and gulping. I had never seen such reactions before. The adolescent girl in Germany of those years must have been under a particularly awful strain.

Finally Elizabeth arrived from Prague, and after a joyful reunion we went to see a major Nazi rally. It was in the Nuremberg stadium, and it couldn't have been better organized or better staged. Both of us were enormously impressed, but unfortunately not enough to restrain our giggles when der Führer finally appeared, striding down the auditorium steps, answering the roaring "Heil Hitler" on every side with a kind of loose-jointed flop of his right forearm. Our insuppressible laughter gained us lots of dirty looks and hissed insults (truly deserved, I suppose—we were certainly being rude and silly). Both of us were frightened on our way out; there were so many people there in uniform or carrying small flags and neither of us had ever been in a hostile crowd before. It was really scary.

We left Nuremberg as soon as we could get a train and pulled into Strasbourg, France, the next morning. What a contrast. There was a farmer's market near the station, and we gorged ourselves on fresh fruit and cucumbers and tomatoes. (Germany had provided us with excellent sausage and bread and beer, but very little green stuff.) Elizabeth then went on to Paris and I to England, where I took a train to Devonshire because I had read about it in so many books and I desperately needed to get somewhere else—anywhere else. I blindly stumbled upon a bed-and-breakfast place run by a motherly woman who let me go to bed upstairs and stay there for a whole week, bringing me pots of tea and bread and butter and letting me read all her children's old books. It was exactly what I needed—a quiet journey into the English past.

Our great trip ended on an Italian liner that left from Trieste. Father and Deanie went first-class, Elizabeth and I farther down. Below first, we discovered that every corner was stuffed with Germans and Austrians going nowhere except away. They were like the men Father saw during the Depression hanging off the Texas trains, going to the end of the line wherever that was, and I felt desperately bad for them. The ship's last European stop was in Lisbon; most of the refugees had to get off there, because it was a free port where they could stay for a limited few months and try to get a visa for somewhere—anywhere—else. I watched the long gray line of them getting off the ship and cried.

One of the older men had taught me a German song that he said his daughter used to sing. I had the sense not to ask too many questions about his family, but I learned the song and he seemed to get pleasure when I sang it to him. He got off the ship at Lisbon and I never saw him again.

> Ee-ah-ho, heute Schimmel, ee-ah-ho
> Unser Weg ist der selbe, so wie so
> Du und ich und überall haben jeder seinen Stall
> Ee-ah-ho, heute Schimmel, ee-ah-ho

I have thought a lot about how I could possibly have made that once-in-a-lifetime trip with so little forethought, so little knowledge, so little research, so little concern with what was going on in the places I was about to see. It was an Ugly American teenager voyage, I'm afraid—no uglier than most seventeen-year-olds would have made then, but still almost completely self-centered and shockingly ill-informed. I had my personal nose rubbed in the reality of Nazism only once, on a train crossing from Czechoslovakia to Germany, when I suddenly realized that in my well-worn guitar case I had sequestered several eight-inch recordings of the Red Army Chorus. (I had never heard better choral singing in my life; I had been knocked over by their depth and sonority.) Then, all of a sudden, I thought about what they might be singing, and I froze in terror that the German *polizei*, coming through inspecting the luggage and seizing upon the "Red Communist" discs, might arrest me for smuggling in seditious literature. I was passed through, of course, but after that I thought much more deeply about the current state of Europe. Nothing like a good scare to focus your attention.

But I do not believe that I was that different from the rest of the United States, really. The experience of World War I, the stock market crash, the Depression, had led our nation to focus tightly on its own problems, and what was then called "isolationism" was a perfectly respectable position. I just wish it hadn't blocked out so much of my own thinking. I had to do a lot of work during the next years to feed my engine back up to a contemporary speed.

⌐⌐

We steamed into New York early in September with just about time for me to do some clothes shopping and get to Pennsylvania. My mother had often talked of Bryn Mawr as a possible collegial home for me: it was an all-women's college near Philadelphia, with a reputation for high standards and tough scholarship. I had little knowledge of the place myself, but I knew that Father and Deanie would offer no objection to my going there. They approved and financed, and so I found myself on a little commuter train, chuffing northward out of Philadelphia to another and different part of the world.

Academically, Bryn Mawr proved to be all and more than I had hoped for. I loved sitting in a carrel in the library with a whole mountain of books under my feet and over my head and nobody telling me what or which I had to read. I loved going out to tea in the twilight with my eyes tired and sitting round a tea shop table with friends, talking about what we were reading or writing. It was the way I had always thought college life ought to be; it made me feel once and for all (I thought) grown up. I loved going to classes, sometimes through snow, always through some beautiful bit of woods or gardens. I loved studying at night in my room, working so hard, enjoying tackling difficult things.

I admired the college's philosophical approach to undergraduate students. Basically, when I was there the administration held that students had selected Bryn Mawr in full knowledge of its intense dedication to the education of women, and surely no one would have registered who did not intend to pursue such an education wholeheartedly and energetically, putting other interests aside for the moment. Translated, that meant that if you wanted to go to New York or Philadelphia for the weekend, you simply left a phone number where you could be reached and went. During your absence, Bryn Mawr was serenely confident that you were going off-campus to work in a particular museum or library—and very much of the time that was the case. (There were students who habitually left campus for other reasons, but I noticed they did not stay with us long.)

The same quiet, rather regal approach was taken to student affairs and general conduct. The general assumption was that a Bryn Mawr student would always behave appropriately, and if she did not there was some overwhelming reason which was probably not the affair of the college. This attitude no doubt resulted in the almost total absence of hullabaloo that greeted my only truly untoward action on the campus. It was all so innocent from my point of view.

Carl Sandburg was to lecture one evening at Bryn Mawr. His arrival was to be in the morning, and he was invited to an honorary tea and dinner at the Deanery before the lecture. I was not invited to any of the festivities except the lecture, but I realized that no one at Bryn Mawr knew that he and my father were good friends or that Sandburg had stayed at our Dallas house frequently (during which visits he always read to me from his *Rootabaga Stories*). I felt that I should show some personal hospitality, and I began to wonder what Father would have liked, coming into a strange college to speak. I knew immediately, when I put it that way, that what Father would have liked was a good drink, probably bourbon. So I trudged to the town, found and bought a vaguely familiar bottle, wrapped it up, and left it for Mr. Sandburg at the Deanery along with a welcoming note, and went on about my business. Later in the afternoon, the word went around the student body that Mr. Sandburg had not come down, either for the tea or the dinner, and had sent only the message that he was very tired.

I apprehensively attended the lecture. He kept the audience of faculty and students waiting until they began to stir restively. Finally the central stage curtains parted with a grand swish and Mr. Sandburg charged to the lectern, pointed an accusing finger at the entire audience seated before him, and thundered, "What do *you know* today—for sure?" Everybody froze. Personally I couldn't think of a single thing, and I doubt, in spite of the college's intensive focus on education and its emphasis on the glorious fact, anybody else could either. He went on turning us inside out along that line for what seemed an endless time and then relaxed, brought out his guitar, and sang us a whole bunch of songs, many of which I already knew.

A reception was set up behind the stage, and I attended along with most of the audience. President Marion Park—a quiet, impeccable lady and a formidable scholar—stood at the door to introduce the eminent speaker. When he caught sight of me, Sandburg grabbed me in an enthusiastic hug and said to Dr. Park, "This is a wonderful young lady you have here; you don't know how lucky you are. I started reading poetry to her when she was no more than five years old. And do you know what she just did for me?

She sent an elegant bottle of whiskey to my room to help me relax and feel welcome on my first trip to Bryn Mawr." Dr. Park never turned a hair. She said, "Mr. Sandburg, we entirely agree with you about Bess and are delighted to have her among our students." I never heard another word about the whole thing.

Thinking back, it seems to me that all three of the active participants in this event behaved according to their own admirable standards. I upheld my family's views on proper hospitality, Sandburg managed to both prod and soothe his sensitive audience and still happily greet his old friend's daughter, and President Park calmly refused to make an issue out of a well-meant but ill-conceived action that would probably never recur. A dicey situation handled well, especially by the experienced Dr. Park.

The Bryn Mawr faculty of my day was also sort of Olympian (to me), and I only remember two teachers with any clarity: my sociology professor, who allowed me to undertake my first field project by going out all alone and studying a small isolated community in the Philadelphia flats (I still have my paper on that adventure); and my anthropology professor, who flunked me on my big term paper in Anthropology I. I was shocked, although I had to agree that I had not done any single part of the project according to her previous careful instructions (but to this day, I still think I had had a good idea). We circled each other somewhat warily after that, but we fell into a good talk at a reunion dinner years later and ended up friends.

My fellow students are more difficult to describe. Bryn Mawr based a lot of annual activities on the different classes—senior, junior, sophomore, and freshman. I had come in during the second year of the class of 1941 and thereby missed out on the first year's bonding activities with my fellow class members. I thus felt little identity with any class and chose my friends from all available ages and groups. And the ages and groups there were raised so differently. For only one example, a contingent of dorm mates once burst into the basement laundry room, where I was peacefully doing my week's wash, complaining that they had been looking for me all over the building with no success. They had never been in the laundry before and inquired how I had been so brave as to find it all by myself. It turned out they all had small cardboard suitcases they would fill up weekly with their dirty clothes and mail back to their family; the clothes would be washed and ironed nicely and returned to them in the same container during the next few days. I found that as astounding as they found my doing my own laundry. Our lives just didn't converge in the parts I would have expected.

Bryn Mawr students, though, were invariably well read, much more worldly-wise than I, and intellectually determined. As a group, they were astonishingly bright. I liked them and I think most of them liked me, in spite of my strange songs and guitar playing and left-wing ideas and queer ways. I managed to learn, I think, from all of them. But one of my best ways of learning was through the freedom Bryn Mawr gave me to go off-campus on brief forays, from which I could always return back safe into the nest without having to go into any detail about what I had been up to. I took full advantage of this: I visited union meetings in downtown Philadelphia, where I was looked at with suspicion but generally allowed to stay and listen; I went to meetings of small local political parties and to many different kinds of churches.

I went to New York, visiting rehearsals of *Back Where I Come From*, the new CBS radio program brother Alan was then doing with his friend Nicholas Ray, staying at his apartment where a few years before I had first met the great singer Aunt Molly Jackson from Harlan County, Kentucky ("Bloody Harlan," they called it then). She was an amazing singer, her great bugling voice and zest for life shining through every word of the old-timey ballads, jokey songs, and picket-line rants she laid on her table for all to hear. I would remember how she belted out "I Hate the Capitalist System" and "Which Side Are You On?" and our trip through Kentucky and the La Follette debates would streak again through my mind. I was studying labor history at Bryn Mawr, and the varied themes of my life were beginning to circle as they do to this day.

And yes, I did go to various museums and libraries in New York every visit, especially the New York Public Library. In fact I remember an especially climactic moment of my growing up that took place in front of the left-hand lion (facing west) of the New York Public Library. I had come out of an afternoon at the library and was walking along Fifth Avenue, when I suddenly thought to myself: "I don't have to be creative if I don't want to!"

And the pressure of the world lifted. I had not realized it was there before. But it all had to do with Mother, and my brother Alan's being so brilliant, and Father's hopes for me, and all my teachers. Suddenly, I realized that they were not in charge of me, I was. What a turnover. What a new world!

FIVE

The Almanacs and the War

My time spent watching rehearsals of *Back Where I Come From* turned out to be some of the most influential hours of my life so far. My brother Alan (script writer and producer) and Nicholas Ray (director) put together a marvelous cast—Burl Ives, the Golden Gate Quartet, Josh White, and Pete Seeger always, with Leadbelly, Woody Guthrie, Aunt Molly Jackson, Sonny Terry, Brownie McGhee, and other now-fabled performers as available. The script was almost entirely composed of what nowadays might be called "folk speech"; it was somewhat Sandburgian in style, with long strings of jokes, proverbs, and hilarious traditional sayings. Each program started off with the statement, "Back where I come from, they always say . . ."—and away the cast would go, outdoing each other in whoppers like "He's so skinny . . ." or "The mosquitoes down here are so big . . ." Nick directed it all briskly with keen enjoyment; in fact everybody was laughing most of the time. And after every show, he and Alan would invite me out for coffee and a postmortem, and always one of the topics would be "Can we possibly keep Pete on the show any longer? He's just so bad, but he's such a sweet fellow and maybe he'll get better." It was true. The other cast members had put in a great deal more performance time than Pete, who was just starting out, and I began to see that one of the things that made for a great performer was simply a lot of performing. As they say, *Faciendo . . .*

Not that Pete didn't play a lot. He practiced so much it could drive a person crazy. If there was an instrument within reach he was tickling it, and if there wasn't he was drumming on the table or trying to see what sounds he could squeeze out of anything lying near. He wasn't ever rude or intrusive; he simply worked away quietly all the time. His voice was accurate and tuneful, but not very strong. When he came back from the army years later he had developed a grown man's voice and energy, and it was a real shot in the arm to hear him. Probably he had just needed time for his long, lean body to pull itself together and for his muscles to solidify and take some shape. When I was teaching, I used to encourage young musicians with this story.

Pete lived in a nearby apartment with Lee Hays, a beautiful bass singer with a great southern repertoire and a great stage presence. Lee was witty and totally engaging; when he waved his great arms at you, it was impossible not to sing with him. Millard Lampell was there too, a slick and sassy lyricist (by far the quickest and cleverest of us all in that department), young and handsome with a long train of girlfriends—never a lead singer, but completely reliable and dedicated. There were others who came in and out, most notably Woody Guthrie from Oklahoma, whose persona and brilliance and total devotion to getting the world to listen to him none of the rest of us ever could match. They were forming a singing group, which they finally christened the Almanac Singers.

There were several unusual things about the Almanac Singers. By the time I joined them, after graduating from Bryn Mawr, they had a clearly announced and presented reason for being: they were going to try to bring the music of the people back to the people. By that, they meant they would sing songs that dealt with contemporary issues and problems, using as vehicles mostly older songs that had also come out of serious and difficult times (reworking them sometimes to fit modern situations). They might also write new songs to speak to special issues. Then they would sing these songs to the audience they believed most needed to hear them—working people first of all. Anybody else was, of course, welcome.

Most of the Almanacs' new repertoire were songs based on classic southern traditional melodies, and they both played and sang in what might today be called "old-timey country," a kind of spin-off of the Carter Family, Jimmie Rodgers, and some of the early blues singers. Overall, they admired and were imitating the best of traditional southern music, both black and white, just the kind of thing that Alan and my father had been recording. And all of that music was actually brand new to the New York City music scene at that time; it came across as fresh and new, and the youthfulness and enthusiastic energy of the singers themselves helped produce their early popularity. My brother Alan, who admired the work of the Almanacs greatly, said that he felt that the group was learning how to bring country music to the city and doing a whale of a job of it.

Probably my knowledge of the Library of Congress repertory was my biggest contribution to the group. I had an accurate but unreliable singing voice; the role of solo performer was not really comfortable for me, but I did know a lot of good songs. And I got along with everybody, really. The Almanacs, like almost every young musical assemblage I have ever known, were inherently unstable, sometimes quarrelsome, and given to large, off-the-cuff pronouncements on matters of policy that later had to change with the changing times. I was so inexperienced and so busy—I worked regular nine-to-five hours at the New York Public Library and, later on, at the Office of War Information—that, to my relief, I usually wasn't around for the hottest exchanges of the latest disagreement.

We led a style of life that would be totally familiar, I suspect, to any college student of the 1970s or 80s. To keep living expenses to a minimum, we rented a series of large, cheap apartments (installing in each a coin telephone so that we wouldn't run up huge telephone bills), divided up the bedroom and living spaces according to who was going to be around when, and set about our various life styles with little alteration, I suspect, except there was always somebody around to play some music with. Saturdays and Sundays we would host open concerts in a big bare room next door, where for a small contribution people could come and go and listen to any of the musicians who chose to come round and join us—maybe Leadbelly or Burl Ives or Josh White. Lee Hayes suggested we call these amorphous affairs "hootenannies," and they helped us keep going fiscally and professionally. Then, when we weren't playing or singing in our varied combinations, we could always have what we hopefully referred to as "organizing meetings," during which we would debate our various problems (mostly concerning getting bookings). Other than that, people were pretty much on their own.

We did go out as often as we could arrange it to sing at union meetings and social events, such as dances and small concerts. We almost always accepted every invitation to sing anywhere—we needed the money too badly to turn anything down—and thereby managed to double- and even triple-book ourselves on popular evenings, forcing us to dash wildly from Queens to Brooklyn and far Yonkers, sometimes dividing ourselves in two (a procedure that caused our audiences some irritation, since they had come expecting to hear a group including Pete Seeger or Lee Hays or Woody Guthrie, and a nondescript bunch of leftover Almanacs would turn up instead). But we had the songs to fall back on, and audiences were pretty tolerant those days because we were working on a way of presenting these interesting and new-ish songs that was itself new and diverting. There had been other city-based traveling singers before (Richard Dyer-Bennet and Henrietta Yurchenko come immediately to mind), but we were young and sassy and varied and cheerfully out to change the world. We were full of jokes and could often "make up" a whole song about our audience and their particular problems right there on the spot.

We never wore costumes or any other distinguishing marker, but just attended bookings in the clothes we had on. Indeed, during one of our out-of-town bookings for a national union, an old gentleman came up and said kindly, "I'd just like to point out one thing to you. When we go out for an evening, even just to a union meeting, we clean up and dress up a bit so as to present ourselves well. And when you youngsters come in here in jeans and with your hair not combed it makes us feel like you don't think we were worth your dressing up for." Now that was a shocker, and it took up a number of organizing meetings. We never did dress formally or adopt a costume, but I do think we all took a little more pains to look presentable.

In the middle of all of this, I fell in love. Both Peter and Baldwin Hawes, brothers, had become sort of in-and-out members of the Almanacs. Peter was the older by two years; he was very interested in the political concerns of the times and finally, after shipping out on fruit boats to Puerto Rico for several years, he took the plunge and moved to the island, taking with him his charming wife, Ellen, who also frequented the Almanacs house from time to time. Baldwin, my true love, had received the nickname "Butch" when he was a husky toddler in a striped jersey; he later became very slim indeed, and we variously searched for some time for a more dignified and appropriate name, but we never found one. (Beware of the casual nickname—sometimes it just won't leave you alone.) Butch was an excellent visual artist, but he functioned in the Almanacs primarily as a songwriter and first-class guitar backup. Woody said frequently that he preferred Butch to back him up more than anybody else in the group, except possibly for Cisco Houston (another name I haven't mentioned), a fine musician who dropped in from time to time.

I had only begun working with the Almanac Singers on a "full-time" basis in June 1941, when international concerns were beginning to dominate the public conversation. It was a frightening time. Every day, it seemed, another once-stable European political reality would fall to the rapidly expanding Nazi armies, and the agonies of the death camps were beginning to reach our ears. The Almanacs, as self-defined commentators, were inevitably affected by the intense national debate between the "warmongers" and the "isolationists" (and the points between). Before every booking, we had to decide: were we going to sing some of our hardest-hitting and most eloquent songs, all of which were antiwar, and if we weren't, what would we sing anyway? More and more, we found ourselves substituting an older song repertoire where, we hoped, the next headline would not challenge our entire roster of poetic ideas. Woody Guthrie wrote a song that mournfully stated, "I started out to write a song to the entire population / But no sooner than I got the words wrote down, here come a brand-new situation."

The Almanacs in toto were embedded in almost never-ending argumentation, debate, and planning meetings, and I myself was struggling with my old pacifist convictions. Vital to our actual survival was the arrival of Sis Cunningham and Gordon Friesen, experienced picket line and progressive cause workers from Oklahoma. In addition to their strong musical repertoires, they brought the group a kind of grown-up stability that was very important during the later years of the war, when so many of the fellows in the group were drafted or went into the wartime merchant marine. And it was the breaking up of personnel that finally got us.

The Almanacs lasted only two or three years—a pretty good run for any performing group over the long haul—but they proved to be extraordinarily influential. Several highly successful commercial performing groups, some involving ex-members, based themselves on the group (notably the Weavers with Pete Seeger and Lee Hays), and small, mostly local Almanacs-type organizations still spring up across the country. We made few headlines during the peak of our singing period, but there were surely many afterward.

My own explanation for the remarkable effectiveness of the Almanac Singers is that they stayed with their initial ideas: to base their work on the problems of the period in which they were singing, to perform their music within a country ballad/string band style (heavily influenced by African American musical ideas), to foster a kind of informal "everybody sing in" kind of audience participation, and to extend the base for an entirely different way of listening to music.

Actually, being an Almanac was not really a full-time occupation unless you were a songwriter or a professional musician. I held at least two other fascinating jobs during that period; it was relatively easy to find work then because when the United States entered the war a labor shortage quickly developed. My first job was at the great New York Public Library, where I became one of Dr. Carleton Sprague Smith's three secretaries for a time. Dr. Smith was head of the Music Department and an energetic, creative, and well-organized man. The most experienced of his secretaries took care of his blooming correspondence on matters to do primarily with library science and the general affairs of the ethnomusicological world. The second secretary, able both to speak and write in fluent Spanish and Portuguese, handled an equally large correspondence with Latin American musicians and musicologists. Dr. Smith was a forerunner in arranging exchanges of U.S. and Latin American classical composers and performers, an activity that put him in touch with symphony orchestras, opera companies, and music publishers all over the hemisphere. At the time, his was an early attempt to put the art worlds of the major continents together, and Dr. Smith took particular pride in having his letters to Brazil go out in impeccable Portuguese and his letters to Peru and Argentina go out in equally literate Spanish.

My job was a distant third: I was charged with taking care of the paperwork concerned with the CBS Radio *School of the Air,* a first-time ever (I believe) educational series that was played every day in thousands of elementary school rooms across the country. Most of my work involved locating published sources for CBS's copyright clearance department. Dr. Smith cheerfully scheduled hundreds of traditional song performances to illustrate his lectures, and I found myself becoming known in limited circles at CBS as an "authority" (shades of my initiation under Father and Alan all those years ago). On one memorable occasion when an African chant was to be played, I was stationed in the actual director's booth during the live broadcast with my finger on an "off the air" button, instructed to press it if I recognized even a few notes that might have been copyrighted. On less steamy days, I also gathered up research books and papers necessary for the weekly scripts. It was a very educational and rewarding job that ended too soon. After December 1941, CBS gradually ceased broadcasting all not-for-profit programs not directly addressing wartime issues and the *School of the Air* was discontinued.

And then, on January 30, 1943, Butch and I got married. A sample of our delight and determination to get off to a good start was reflected in an early conversation I recall about how we would live. I pointed out that I had a portable typewriter to contribute to our future; Butch proudly matched that with his ownership of a *Webster's Collegiate Dictionary* (fifth edition, and practically brand-new). We hugged each other, joyfully convinced that we had already equipped ourselves with the basic necessities for a happy life. We moved out of Almanac House (although we continued singing as Almanacs when we could) and found a one-bedroom apartment on Perry Street in Greenwich Village, with easy access to a number of small music clubs then showcasing the great jazz musicians pouring into New York from the South and the Midwest. Sidney Bechet, Billie Holiday, Pee Wee Russell—we could hear them all night long for the price of one rum-and-coke, which we split. Daytimes, Butch got a scholarship at a well-known school of photography, and I went off to a new job at the Office of War Information (OWI) on Columbus Circle.

Things moved rather swiftly in those years. The OWI was a sudden attempt by the federal government to provide the world with official information as to what was going on from the point of view of the United States. The national agency was set up as a tripartite being: the central office in Washington, D.C., and two active units, one on the West Coast in California and the other at Columbus Circle in New York. The West Coast office was empowered to take care of communication needs with the eastern theater of the war, and the East Coast office with those of the western theater. I had never heard of the OWI when I started on my new job as assistant to Nicholas Ray, then special projects director for the western theater, which included the western and eastern Mediterranean, the whole of Europe, and all Africa. Our basic duty was to get as much official information into these areas as fast we could, the quickest and most desirable medium being radio.

Essentially, the Columbus Circle office I worked in operated as a broad-cast station, but with a few special problems of its own. We were on the air twenty-four hours a day in all of the languages in our far-flung region for which speakers could be located. At the time I came on board, our broad-casts to Africa were limited to the South African Republic (in English and Afrikaans, if we could find an intelligible speaker) and a few of the African nations bordering on the Mediterranean, especially Egypt and Saudi Arabia. Our major means of broadcasting was through short-wave radio, a very weak reed at its best: static was horrible, and listening even in France was almost impossible, as our underground reporters told us. The BBC was also broadcasting from England, and we had difficulty not duplicating its efforts. But we soldiered on—in French, Flemish, Polish, Czech, Portuguese, and Arabic (among others)—providing, as we could, interesting programming for local broadcasting stations in unoccupied areas.

Most of our programs were straight news, heralded by a brisk and cheerful fife and drum band rendition of the first two lines of "Yankee Doodle." Somewhere in my inchoate years at the OWI I was informed from "upstairs" that various underground groups in Europe wanted us to change our musical theme, since when they were listening in utmost secrecy for our broadcasts its rambunctious "Yankee Doodle came to town" made it immediately perceptible to any passersby that the USA was on the air. Could we please, they asked, give them something less noticeable? The powers that be powered, and I was instructed to obtain a celeste—a small, soft, treble xylophone sometimes used to indicate heaven in film scores—and cause "Yankee Doodle" to be played upon it. Actually I played it myself, bypassing the musicians union, which might well have charged us union fees. Though a strong union woman myself, it did not seem to me that the phrase "Yankee Doodle came to town" played slowly and soulfully on a celeste was worth the attention of a true professional musician. As far as I ever knew, my rendition was played—and maybe even heard—on underground radio stations in France and other nations in the European theater.

But it was recorded, as was every other sound sent out over the air from our office. We used the best technology of the times: sixteen-inch acetate discs—the same kind that Father and Alan had used in their later recordings. Each program was duplicated and reduplicated. Some shows needed to be broadcast to suit various time zones, some shows needed to be rerecorded in Croatian, or Farsi, or some other local language and then broadcast—all on these outsized, fragile discs produced under enormous tension and labeled by an assistant who couldn't speak very good English. They got lost, they got misfiled, they got broken, they got taken to the wrong studio by someone who was trying to be helpful.

Someone was needed to set up a proper record library to keep all our precious discs in order, so I was assigned to set it up and run it. As in most radio studios, everything always had to be done immediately and everybody in the building was tired; but every program had to be broadcast during hours appropriate for the local time zone, so the record library had to be staffed twenty-four hours a day. I finally established a rule that no human being other than library personnel could set a foot inside, so great was the disorder and panic that one exhausted and overdriven program director could produce in five minutes.

And then we had our own special tortures. Many news broadcasts were supposed to be copied down by the listeners for wider circulation. Those had to be read at a s-l-o-w dictation pace: the announcers would stand at the microphone saying, "The (pause) High (pause) Com-mand (pause) an-nounced (pause) to-day (pause) that . . ." It was mind-numbing: some announcers actually fell asleep on their feet while reading, script in hand; others lost their places so frequently that somebody else had to stay awake and follow the script with pointing finger. And then if one of those painfully produced recordings got broken or misfiled in the record library, tempers would rise to Balkan heights and tears would flow. My "staff" consisted of several young people (who I think were more like fourteen and fifteen years old and had merrily lied about their ages) and two somewhat unusual lovers of the night watch; none of them earned more than twenty-five dollars a week, with no overtime pay. Among other duties, I was supposed to keep their morale up because substitutions were simply unavailable in those days of the booming war economy.

The Music Department where I worked was constantly on the defensive against the many people who believed, with some justification, that broadcasting *music* over short-wave was foolhardy and hopeless and money down a rat hole. We fought back vigorously, pointing out that the Allies were trying to win the hearts, minds, and souls of both the occupied and unoccupied nations, so we must show ourselves, as a nation, to be cultured and open not only to technology and representative government, but to the arts as well.

The OWI had obtained permission from all of the appropriate musical organizations to broadcast any American musical record without fees throughout the war. But in broadcasting to the Union of South Africa should we use the classic Paul Robeson recorded performance of "Ballad for Americans" or that of Bing Crosby, whose enunciation was crisper? There were those who said that if the Robeson version was played, all Afrikaans receiving stations would turn us off; others held that part of our job was to present American music at its most exciting best. Another typical problem: should we broadcast the famous Chopin prelude celebrating the freedom of Poland from czarist Russia to Warsaw and other European capitals during the fierce fighting over Prague in the final days of the war while the Soviet Army were still in there fighting? Who were on which side when, and how were they to be identified? Clearly, we were only a tiny part of it, but this was the Good War and the war we all wanted to "win." By doing so, we were going to change the world and make it better, and somehow some small part of all this effort was strongly influenced by music—the emotional part that so often goes unnoticed.

After a few years of facing such insoluble problems, I felt firmly that there was no possible way in which music could ever be thought of as nonpolitical. It was chameleonlike, but it inevitably lent its emotional authority to every context in which it occurred. So we should be careful with this powerful element—we should learn more about how it works and use it joyously, but with considerable respect.

The OWI did have one other major way of broadcasting music: we were authorized to help supply local radio networks and stations in our overseas area with equipment and with material they could rebroadcast according to their own wishes. Many areas of Europe and Africa were experiencing a significant shortage of commercial musical recordings—those eight- and ten-inch discs that were played on home Victrolas. The German record-pressing plants had closed down early in the war, reestablishment of facilities in Greece and northern Africa had been wiped out as well, and local radio stations were suffering from having to use badly scratched, worn-out recordings in order to send out any music at all. We got a request from Washington to provide a source for purchasing what were referred to as "Arab" recordings in considerable quantity to be sent to broadcast stations in the North African countries. This was a bit of a problem, because we were used to providing standard American music and classical music, but who knew this Arabic stuff?

As usual, such unlikely problems were turned over to "the barefoot division," as Nicholas Ray's and my office was originally dubbed. Nick had by then gone on to his later distinguished filmmaking career, so I took a shot at the problem, looking first in the telephone book for record stores that might give me a tip or two. I had never heard any Arabic music in my entire life and was a little vague, like most Americans, on just who spoke Arabic in which countries. In the course of visiting the likely sounding shops, I finally managed to get out to Queens, if I'm not mistaken, and walked into a small, dark store absolutely jammed with records labeled in what I assumed to be Arabic script. (Anyway, I couldn't read it.) A pleasant gentleman came to meet me and we settled down to a pleasant conversation, in the course of which he provided me with tea, served exotically in a glass, and courteously kept from me his undoubted surprise at having a twenty-two-year-old Anglo-Saxon girl breeze into his establishment and start arrangements for a large purchase order from the federal government. He played me some lovely music, too, and explained to my uncomprehending ears where the action was in Egyptian popular song and similar repertories. I went back home, turned in my report, and settled back to wait for the next improbable request.

It seems totally incomprehensible now that a step of such cultural authority could have been handled so casually by someone so unqualified. But at the time, even with my unusual background, I didn't know anybody who could have handled this unexpected chore. Later, the composer Henry Cowell came to direct the OWI Music Division and opened my eyes a bit to the vast areas of non-Western music of which I was totally ignorant.

I need to tell one more improbable episode—again, it was in answer to a specific request from the State Department. The then shah of Iran had been impressed by the physical vitality and excellent conditioning of the American troops he had seen, and he had asked for a physical conditioning program that His Majesty himself could sponsor. Iran, at that time, was a wavering ally, and so an appropriate set of physical jerks was served up in Washington posthaste. They were so successful that the shah decided that all Iranians could share in their benefits (again on the double). The State Department sent the problem to the Music Division, and Henry Cowell—a delightful and sophisticated man with a large collection of Iranian records from his earlier international concertizing—set happily to work on an accompanying musical score with a copy of the U.S. Army physical regulations in one hand and his transcriptions of Iranian traditional themes in the other. Our productions were to be broadcast all over Iran and all citizens urged to participate. (Even I wondered how many Iranians would be in good enough physical condition to undertake a set of army exercises.)

Henry came up with a score requiring a flutist, a cellist, and a drummer, as I recall. That problem was turned over routinely to the local musicians union, while I was instructed to locate a Farsi-speaking announcer who could also physically perform the actions in order to keep the pacing appropriate. This turned out to be a difficult task: the production office had already turned New York upside down trying to locate any announcers fluent in Farsi for our regular newscasts. Either there was a remarkably small population of Iranians in New York at the time or they didn't want to identify themselves. Anyway, one gentleman finally consented after all kinds of patriotic urgings from the State Department.

So, the morning of the recording, four newcomers turned up in the studio: three ill-tempered Musicians Union Local 802 members—hauling their instruments and looking disgustedly at the complex scores Henry handed out—and one slender, pale, reluctant young Persian (as we used to call them) who was absolutely horrified at the notion that he was going to have to perform any physical movement whatsoever. He was an *announcer*, after all. It looked like a long morning to me.

Henry unflaggingly showered the room with his twinkling charm, enough to melt the hearts of any but the four stony egocentrics we had to work with, but to no avail. The Persian gentleman breathed heavily during and after every exercise and at one time announced he was going to faint. Finally, we allowed him to call on a friend to come over and relieve him, and by their taking turns (one counting and one exercising) we finally completed one of the more unusual projects I had ever taken part in. I never have been able to discover if any such recordings were ever broadcast in Iran, but I hope that Henry's beautiful music somehow survived the war and is a part of his legacy. And you can't say we didn't try.

It may seem that I am expending too much time and paper on my days at the OWI, but I have found few people aware of its existence, either then or now. Historically, it followed the WPA (Works Progress Administration) with another attempt by the federal government to bring the ordinary citizen into the flow of communication, which was growing faster every day— including the presentation of art for the people, rather than exclusively for classical concert goers or the music industry. As such, I think, it deserves great respect and attention, even from such an unimportant worker as I then was. In the layers of staff above me, there were some eminent figures; indeed, the head of the entire eastern OWI broadcasting office was the director, actor, and producer John Houseman.

SIX

Boston, Babies, and Beginning to Teach

I left the OWI in 1946 for what was intended as a pregnancy leave and somehow or other I never got back. As far as I know, my employment record is still active in the federal files. But during 1945 the overall situation had begun to change: the United States began its long, paranoid search for spies in sheep's clothing, the irrational term "un-American" became popular, and investigatory activities became ever more frequent and ever more inefficient.

I came home from work one day to discover my unflappable husband a bit shaken by the fact that his afternoon working at home had been interrupted by three separate and independent investigators—one from the Civil Service Commission, one from the FBI, and the third from naval intelligence—all soliciting our view on the loyalty of a gentleman who lived in our apartment building and whom we had never met. Each "intelligence" agent came separately, but two overlapped in our living room and greeted each other with joyful cries and hugs. (They had met while attending several spy-locating classes together.) When all but one had cleared out, the last one turned to Butch and said, "I didn't want to put those fellows down, but they're going about this all wrong. People in New York apartment houses never know each other. What they ought to do is go look in the trash chutes. *That's* where the stuff really is."

It was obvious that I would soon be pursued myself. I had a well-known brother whose political sentiments had been, along with mine, quite public; and I was also chairing the OWI Federal Workers Union Grievance Committee and trying to straighten out such dangerous situations as that of a young Hungarian refugee lady who proudly affirmed in a loyalty interview that she indeed had had extremely close personal relations with many other OWI workers. (She had been dismissed immediately.) It was becoming difficult to know what to do when civil service agents came around to interview me in my working office. They always wanted to learn my views on the loyalty of this or that other employee; since at the time my own loyalty was under question, no matter how I answered it could be taken wrong. I never could figure out how I ought to handle this.

Eventually the bell tolled for me as it had for so many others, and I went down to spend a day in Washington being yelled at by a Civil Service Commission prosecutor who behaved like a bull in heat and had absolutely no manners. I, in turn, went into my upper-class southern lady persona, and we spent a most unpleasant afternoon glaring at each other in front of a few other people whose names and positions I was never told.

I was temporarily dismissed, and I returned to New York to send for those materials in my dossier from which my interrogator had taken his questions. It was terribly discouraging to discover that almost all of the "factual" information against me was simply wrong: dates, addresses, all the things I had assumed investigators would really look for and study. It would have taken me a year or so to properly unwind all the factual knots these inefficient people had drawn around me. And it was also disturbing to discover that two FBI men had gone all the way to Upper Michigan in the middle of the winter to try to question locals about my activities during a summer when I had spent six weeks counseling at a girls' camp. No one in Michigamme had the least notion who I was (the camp was way out in the woods), but I was told the next summer that trying to figure out what I could have been up to besides teaching children to swim had provided considerable amusement to the few permanent residents of the area during the long winter. But the waste of it all. The sheer stupidity. Even if I had been some kind of dastardly villain, what could I have been doing in those far woods?

Then the war was over, the OWI was beginning to close down, and Butch and I had a beautiful baby girl, Corey. Butch had been diagnosed with an acute form of spinal rheumatoid arthritis from which he was to suffer the rest of his life. For now, it was obvious that he could no longer handle the heavy photographic equipment he so adored. He began soliciting graphic art work (he had attended art school before we met), visiting all manner of local publications and building an amusing and thoroughly personal black-and-white illustrative/decorative style that sold modestly. Finally, he was invited by a Boston book publisher to illustrate a forthcoming book. This decided us: it was time for a change. We would leave New York and establish our new family in Boston, where the two Hawes boys' home had been long ago. (Incidentally, I never heard anything further from the U.S. government—nor did they from me, until 1975.)

We moved to Cambridge early in 1947. By then, it was clear to us that we were outstanding procreators and parents, and I was already pregnant with our second child, who turned out to be another superb daughter, Naomi. She taught me (among many other useful lessons) that it is not only heredity or nurturance or both that shapes a baby's personality, but some kind of factor X that must be counted into the procedure. Each one of our eventual three children turned out fascinating, delightful, unmistakably their own person, different from all others.

Due to the terrible postwar housing shortage, when we had to leave our temporary Cambridge quarters we could find only a cold-water flat (no heating whatever) on the wrong side of Beacon Hill in Boston. I will not go into detail about what living without heat can do to the normal human being, but one afternoon the girls' crying roused me to the fact that I had been standing in front of the old iron cooking stove in the kitchen for some two hours, doing absolutely nothing but warming my freezing back half. We had settled in for what proved to be a long bitter-cold winter before we discovered that the nice folks with their own two children living in the building next door were themselves radicals. The father, Otis Hood, was for many years the chairman of the Massachusetts Communist Party. How that inquisitor for the Civil Service Commission would have enjoyed "discovering" that! They turned out to be helpful and friendly neighbors, and after Otis's death I corresponded with his wife for many years.

My father died during the winter of 1947–48. I was already pregnant for the third—and last—time and could not travel to the funeral (the Boston airport was closed because of snow and ice storms anyway). In spite of the many raging past ups and downs between my father and me, he did not forget us, bequeathing us enough money that we were able to make cautious down payments on one-half of a Cambridge duplex and on our first car: a passenger-style Jeep that we drove for some twenty-five years.

With three children so close together—our son, Nick, was born in late summer 1948—we found ourselves pretty well occupied for the next several years. What little spare time we had we spent working for the Progressive Party, which had made a respectable national third-party showing in 1948 and continued to be active in many states, including Massachusetts. We found a lively group of Progressive Party-ers of about our age and joined them with real pleasure. Butch worked mostly on illustrations and cartoons for leaflets; I joined in on helping work up songs for the sound trucks to use in local election campaigns. The idea was to outfit small trucks to cruise slowly through the streets in various political districts attracting listeners for the candidate's speeches. There was absolutely no money for such activities; live volunteer singers were used as far as possible, and they themselves were responsible for coming up with attractive and amusing songs.

I sang on the trucks as much as I could, but babysitting was always a problem and I spent more time at home working on improving the song repertoire. My Almanacs experience came in very handy here, and one day I thought of doing another version of a classic and frequently parodied song, "The Wreck of the Old Ninety-Seven." Pete Seeger had once produced a very funny rewrite for a New York City Transit Workers Union rally that started out:

> Let me tell you the story of some politicians
> Who rode on a yellow scab train
> On a Monday morning they left the station
> And they never were seen again.
> Did they ever return? No, they never returned . . .

My fellow parodist Jacqueline Steiner and I decided it might be fun to redo this in a special Boston context, for the Boston mayor had recently decreed that fares would not be collected when passengers got on but when they got off (so as to be able to charge more for the longer rides). We got to work and jointly came up with "Charley on the MTA" (Metropolitan Transit Authority), which was duly sung on many sound truck runs. It passed quickly out of our attention, since we were always being asked to write more and more.

It was a funny song though, and various singers began to pick it up (this was in the early period of the so-called folksong revival). Finally the Kingston Trio heard it and added it to their repertoire. Jackie and I were amused and pleased but had other things to occupy ourselves with, until one day a gentleman called me from a music publisher and said the Kingston Trio would like to record the song for an upcoming album and could I please give him the copyright data. I said it had never been copyrighted. There was a long silence. (Copyrighting that song had never occurred to either Jackie or me; I personally had not considered it to be anything but a campaign song and continued to think of it that way for some time.) The gentleman finally said slowly that he would consult with his lawyers. And then we got involved in various legalities that resulted finally in the song being copyrighted properly to both Jackie and me. I hadn't understood the fact that it was cheaper for music publishers to ascribe authors and composers to these stray kinds of songs, so as not to become enmeshed in later legal problems.

One final episode. During a much later conversation with the pleasant publisher, he made some remark about possibly changing the last couplet of the final verse—I forget now how or why. I responded that that would require leaving out candidate Wally O'Brien's name, and that seemed a shame since he was such a nice fellow. "Do you mean that Walter A. O'Brien was a real person?" he practically shouted. "He certainly was, or why would we have written a song for his campaign? Okay, he lost—but he did mighty well for a first-timer. We were proud of him," I replied. By now the man was practically screaming. "Good God, he could sue us for infringing on his privacy! Get him out of there!" I still had not internalized the principle that this was no longer a local campaign song; it was now in the same category as "Blue Moon" or "Mairzy Doats" or any other popular song you might think of. We reluctantly "got him out of there," substituting "Get together with your neighbors to fight the fare increase . . ." for "Vote for Walter A. O'Brien to fight . . ." It still seems a shame.

Jackie and I have been receiving royalty checks from "Charley" for many years now, and I at least still feel awkward about them (although the money is fine and I hope I have put it to good use). To me, however, this is a great example of the many joys and advantages of working within a not-for-profit context. If you cast your bread freely and happily on the waters, you may not only, after many days, find it again, but every now and then you may find even more.

For the next several years, the Hawes family just stayed put except for one major expedition on Butch's part. He had been commissioned by the Puerto Rico Board of Education to illustrate a new primer in Spanish for the local public school system, and he visited the island for some three weeks photographing Puerto Rican houses and the general look of the countryside and cities, noting what colors the children seemed to wear most, what kind of schools they went to, all the details he might need to know in order to make appropriate illustrations. It turned out that this was not only a new primer, it was the first primary school book that had ever been published *in Spanish* for Puerto Rican children. We were all terribly proud of the honor.

Back home, I was spending the little spare time I had on Progressive Party neighborhood work, helping organize local door-to-door campaigns on various issues—there was a lot going on in that period. At one point the Cambridge group decided to ask Paul Robeson to do a benefit concert for us at a local church. Mr. Robeson kindly consented; we notified the press of the upcoming extraordinary event and began organizing ticket sales. Then an enormous hullabaloo blew up out of nowhere. Articles were printed all over Boston saying that this horrible Communist singer Paul Robeson was going to invade Massachusetts and there would be mass protests and we should be braced for trouble, possibly even riots. The police called to assure us they would be on hand to keep order, but the church began to get frightened and we were terrified. An experienced organizer from Mr. Robeson's New York office swiftly joined us; he calmly said that Robeson *never* failed to appear at his scheduled events and then gave us useful suggestions for coping with the stormy conditions. After the concert had been sung in the church without incident before a serious and receptive audience (although unheard by the squads of broadcasters and newspaper reporters), he gave us a final few words of advice: "I know you white liberal Progressive Party people. You work at your jobs or at home all day, and then you go to work on political problems. But the black people in Boston and Cambridge think that you are doing what *they* would be doing after a tough day. Most of them think you're having a party and you haven't invited them." I learned more from those few sentences about cultural differences than I had in all my sociology classes at Bryn Mawr.

Actually, I mostly stayed home and kept up with the kids as well as I could, gradually inserting them into nursery schools as they became old enough. The nursery school we liked best, and stayed with, was run by a generous and extremely intelligent African American woman at a church on the wrong side of Cambridge. Both the area and the school were dirt poor, but we weren't especially well off either and fit in nicely with the other school families (mostly Harvard and MIT graduate school students). Tuition for the preschoolers was extremely low, and all parents were asked to help the single teacher out as often as we possibly could.

I began my service by taking my guitar and singing casually to and with the children out in the play yard, where I found myself one day sitting on the board rim around the large sandbox and starting in on a jolly little Bahamian dance tune my brother had recorded years before:

> Don't you hurry worry with me
> Don't you hurry worry with me
> Don't you hurry worry with me
> I'm gonna pack up your eyes with sand

I had already gotten the last phrase out before I quite remembered what it said, and then I was so transfixed with horror that I just went on and sang the next verse (even worse):

> If you tell me that again
> If you tell me that again
> If you tell me that again
> I'm gonna pack up your eyes with sand

The children were watching me steadily with total attention. Nobody moved. Well, I was in for it now, so I just went on and finished the song:

> Mister Munson he got drunk
> Mister Munson he got drunk
> Mister Munson he got drunk
> I'm gonna pack up your eyes with sand

Then I segued directly and thankfully into another Bahamian dance tune about ships in a storm:

> The wind blow east, the wind blow west
> The wind blow the *Sunshine* right down in town
> And the wind blow the *Setting Star* right down in town
> And the wind blow the *China* right down in town . . .

Everyone turned back to sand castle construction. Not a grain of sand had fallen during the song. The iron law of the playground—*Don't throw sand!*—had held. Against a rigorous cultural rule, art had been bested, and I was pretty glad of it just then.

I kept on wandering into the school and singing, and some of the other mothers began to ask me to teach them some of the songs I knew and even how to play the guitar. The folksong revival was underway in New York, and these Boston ladies were intrigued by what seemed to them a novel world of music that looked (and was) pretty simple—at least the way I did it. I finally came up with a trial plan. I knew none of them had the money to buy instruments, so I said I would try to teach them to play a little bit on any fretted stringed instrument they could locate. I suggested they canvass their neighbors to see if any of them didn't have an old guitar or especially a five-stringed banjo sitting in the attic that could be borrowed for the class period. The classic Fairbanks and Cole Company of Boston, whose banjos are still famous, had gone out of business only comparatively recently, and with luck some of their fine instruments might turn up. I also knew that Boston had mothered the creation of a number of cross-bred instruments that nobody played any more—banjolins (banjo/mandolins), twelve- and fifteen-stringed guitars, and the like.

I could play a little guitar and a little five-string banjo and a little mandolin, so I figured I could come up with a reasonable tuning for these folks no matter what instrument they came in with. We would meet once a week, when each one should pay me fifty cents a lesson, of which I would keep twenty-five cents for babysitting expenses and donate the rest to the school. I expected we might go on for maybe a month or two. I also expected a class of five to eight to start.

Arriving with, as loaners for the evening, every instrument we had in the house, I was staggered to see a good twenty-five women, armed with every kind of stringed instrument under the sun, happily expecting me. I took a deep breath and started out to try to get at least most of us approximately in tune. Some instruments had broken strings, some had no strings at all, some gave me no clue as to how they might have been tuned originally. I just laid hands on each one and did the best I could, winding up with at least most of them passibly playable. (The ones I had no idea how to handle, I simply tuned up in either banjo or mandolin tuning and pretended that was the way they should be.) Neighbors gave each other turns at their instruments, and by the end of the evening everyone had gotten to whang away on something

that made a recognizable sound while we sang another exciting round of our song du jour—"Polly Wolly Doodle All Day." I explained that we should all sing loudly, and we did. Actually it was a lot of fun.

That first night it didn't impress me especially that all the banjos were brought in by white mothers, while all the black mothers produced some variety of guitar. This was a truly biracial nursery school (to use the terminology of the time) and there were about equal numbers from each group. I decided that the African American women were simply not willing to be seen playing any kind of minstrel-show-associated music maker, and I was very pleased months later to have several come in with banjos that their mother had "just discovered" in the attic. They had found they liked the sound, and they turned out to be good banjo pickers, too. It's very heartening to see cultural tensions relaxing a bit right in front of your eyes.

This first class we had turned out to be pivotal in my later teaching development. I have since changed the details (what songs to sing, which keys to teach when) many times, but I have never found great need to change my original basic principles when working with beginners—always my specialty. My main strategy with them was to teach for early success and self-approval using large groups (neighbors will always drown out fumbling mistakes), urging loud and enthusiastic singing (for the same purpose), and helping people learn how to listen. It is astounding how many people never listen to—or really hear—the sounds they are producing. I always used only the most skeletal song sheets because I began to feel that somewhere in the first grade they had learned to turn their ears off when their eyes went into action. Maybe dividing up your senses is necessary in order to learn the neural task of reading, but I hope not. Anyway, in my huge classes (later as many as fifty students) I would occasionally and unexpectedly just turn off the lights, and everyone would have to work by the light of their ears and the strength of their neighbors. And after just a little bit they sounded great.

I spent a lot of time and care picking out songs. The first session was almost always devoted to good old "Polly" because it had the longest time between chord changes. After class I would suggest they also try out any simple tune they knew, beginning with the first chord they had learned and—when that started to sound bad—changing to the other one. They had a fifty-fifty chance of being right. And if both of the chords sounded bad, they could change the tune, preferably to "Go Tell Aunt Nancy." In the second class I gave them the magical third chord with which they could accompany hundreds of songs. From then on they learned at least two new songs per session, selected for singability, possibilities for vocal harmonies, stylistic variety, and the fact that I liked to sing them myself.

For the real feature of my teaching style was repetition, which I learned to disguise in a number of ways. Adults proved amenable to my tricks if I could make them seem like fun, but children were very properly too freethinking and playful to put up with them. (And teenagers, I discovered, were apt to have practiced almost continuously since the last class and wanted far more than I was ever prepared to give them.) But a solid adult class would happily sing every song we knew over and over and over until the music was really beginning to sound pretty good.

In my first class at the nursery school, the church janitor/handyman—an agreeable gentleman who, it turned out, had played with a Dixieland combo in his younger days—used to drop by from time to time. When I would ask him how he thought I was doing with the class, he always said the same thing: "Pretty good, but too fast. One song, one hour. One song, one hour." As the class went along, I began to see the strength of his position. When you've done something often enough so that you've solved all the technical problems and plumbed what emotional depths you can find, you will begin to relax into freer playing (which is always more musical) and maybe even try a new little finger wiggle here and there just to relieve the monotony. I think he was teaching me where the art of improvisation is born.

Bess Bauman Brown, 1897.

John Avery Lomax in his office at the University of Texas, Austin.

John Avery Lomax (with chicken and cat), Prince (dog), Shirley, and Bess Brown Lomax, College Station, Texas, 1906–7.

Alan, Bess Brown Lomax, and Bess

Bess Lomax in Girl Scout uniform, Lubbock, Texas, c. 1931.

Some Almanac Singers. From left: Woody Guthrie, Millard Lampell, Bess Lomax, Pete Seeger, Arthur Stern, and Sis Cunningham.

Almanac Singers: Bess Lomax, Butch Hawes, Arthur Stern, Charles Polachek, Detroit, 1943.

Bess in the Almanac days.

Bess, Naomi, Nick, Corey, and Butch Hawes at the home of Butch's parents in Bolton, Massachusetts, before leaving for California, 1950.

Bess and Butch, Santa Monica, California, late 1950s.

Hawes family Christmas card, a linoleum print by Butch, Santa Monica, California.

SEVEN

California and More Teaching

That wonderful nursery school class, during which I learned so much, went on for a year or so, as I recall. Our children kept on growing and we kept on trying to raise them up and keep some food on the table; but good book-publishing jobs were getting fewer and fewer, and Butch was getting less and less physically able to hit the streets and sell his drawings to local newspapers and newsletter printers. The winters continued bitter cold. I picked up Butch's overcoat one day and it almost made me stagger, it was so heavy. The children kept on getting bronchitis and childhood pneumonias and ear infections, and we began to feel that New England, although we all loved it, could not continue to be home base for us. At that time, we simply were not a sturdy family.

In those days, book publishing (always Butch's love) was centered in New York, Boston, and Los Angeles/San Francisco. We decided to try our luck in California as so many had before us, and in early 1951 we started our own migration. Selling the house (what we owned of it) provided us with a stake, and we kept telling ourselves that if we were going to be broke, we could at least be broke and warm instead of broke and cold. It was quite an odyssey. We pared our belongings down as far as we could and sent them off by moving van, including the backseat of the Jeep. The empty Jeep body was padded with mattresses off the children's beds and all the pillows in the house, thereby turning it into an enlarged playpen with suitcase and toy-box walls. The top of the patient Jeep was loaded down with additional vital possessions tied on with ropes, and we took off—Butch driving, me in charge of meals and morale.

We started off south hoping for warmer weather, made our way down the Appalachians, and then turned right in Louisiana to start the long trek across the continent, stopping for a few days in Texas for a visit with my adored sister, with whom I had spent such happy years. As we climbed slowly onto the cap rock before Lubbock, where the retreating fields of ice had paused so many million years ago, Butch said, "You know, whenever I've asked you about the country around Lubbock, you've always said, 'Well, it's the flattest place in the world.' And I've always said back, 'It can't be. Flat is flat; there just can't be anything flatter' . . . but you were right—it *is* flatter than flat."

It took us four days driving to get all the way across Texas. We were simply bound and determined to make Los Angeles, together with our three children (then aged six, four and a half, and three and a half), all the money we had in our pockets, and all our worldly goods in either the Jeep or the moving van. And we didn't know a soul in the place we were heading to, although we did have the name of an arthritis specialist (an accurate indication of our priorities). Our Boston friends had urged us to head for San Francisco, where they knew lots of people from the Progressive Party days, but we stuck with our decision to try our luck where it was *warm*.

We started out in Sunland, a district of Los Angeles we had picked solely because of its name. But we soon found it was not just sunny, but dry, hot, deserty, and generally unappealing. We began a better-informed search and eventually reached someone who actually listened to our story and suggested that we call a realtor named Bob DeWitt, who lived in a place called Topanga Canyon. We called and during the first phone call cemented a friendship that lasted over a good ten years. Bob found us first a rental, and after some months a small house we could afford to buy right across the street from the Will and Herta Geer family. The Geers put us in touch with Matty and Mickey Miller and Richard Dehr and his family, with whom we played music and enjoyed close friendships until we had to leave Topanga in 1955.

Topanga fit our needs and our likes to a T: a rural community full of not-generally-well-off people, artists of all stripes and passions, independent thinkers, and refugees from Hollywood and the multitude of un-American committees. There was a local elementary school; there was a "crick" (often with some water in it) running down to the ocean; and there was always the Geer place, where Will and Herta, whom we had met casually in New York, played in their own makeshift outdoor theater with their friends.

The Geers used every bit of their extensive property for gardening, raising children, and putting on all kinds of local theatrical events. One Sunday noon they reenacted the Lincoln-Douglas debates, with the audience sitting at picnic tables on the house side of the creek, eating picnic food they had brought with them, surrounded by striped bunting and red and blue balloons. The debaters arrived from the highway, one standing in the back of a horse-drawn wagon, the other driving an old-fashioned buggy Will had gotten on loan somewhere. Each was suitably introduced to the spectators, and then the debate began, using the vivid words from the actual event. The audience spontaneously divided themselves into partisans for one man or the other and began cheering and insulting their rivals accordingly. Children ran through the scene, playing in the creek and being scolded by their parents for not paying proper attention to the eminent speakers. It was tremendous fun and deeply moving in view of the political context in which we were living. Will Geer, of course, had been an early victim of the Hollywood blacklist and was completely out of theatrical work until he later landed his famous role on *The Waltons*.

The Geers also often lent their spacious highway location for local folk music concerts and hootenannies, and so Topanga gradually became a temporary stopping-off point for many of the young artists of the then-thriving folksong revival movement. They came in to rest up from the road, to try to land a few musical gigs, and to play music with each other. Woody Guthrie camped out for two years or so at the Geers' and at our place and, finally, alone back in the Topanga hills. Guy Carawan, Frank Hamilton, Vern Partlow, Marcia Berman, Odetta, Jack Elliott, among many others from greater Los Angeles visited and sang often at local concerts. And during this same period Ed Pearl was developing the seminal coffeehouse/night club, the Ash Grove, in West Los Angeles, where musicians could actually get jobs for a week or two. In Topanga Canyon and the nearby San Fernando Valley (when we could locate a caller) Butch would play fiddle and I would play mandolin, along with various of my guitar class members temporarily organized into a square-dance band for impromptu dancing. It was rich country for us: music and friends all over the place.

But, like everything, it had its downsides too. We sometimes felt that we had dragged the poisonous atmosphere created by the continuing Red

Scare of the fifties all the way across the country. The FBI appeared disconcertingly often at our Topanga door, and we had to warn the children not to talk about their parents or our neighbors (the Geers) to anybody, causing us to subtly alter our performance repertoire and, in a deep way, our relationship with our own children. And although we had thankfully left the horrible heavy overcoat in Massachusetts, daily life in Topanga was not exactly physically relaxing. The worst parts were having to haul all potable drinking water and grocery supplies for a family of five up to our hilltop house via a lengthy staircase, and having to drive at least half an hour to get to either Santa Monica or the Valley—twice as long if we were trying to get to Los Angeles proper. And although the weather performed as promised—beautifully warm and dry, with no winter—and Butch's bones were certainly grateful for the change, the arthritis was still there working away, and he was rarely without pain.

⌒

We were mostly an active bunch. We were also very broke and were living in a ridiculously small house, probably originally built for a weekend getaway cottage. Butch and I slept in the big bed on the side porch; the three children in bunk beds in the single bedroom. There was a small living room, a minute kitchen, and a bath with only a shower stall. The family group was further adorned by the presence of a dog named Quartsy, whom we had bargained for at a local swapping fair by trading several quarts of homemade applesauce for a delightful puppy (thus the name).

When I took Quartsy to the vet for a checkup, he looked sober. We had been too naive to insist on any kind of medical record, and the vet said he didn't think our puppy had had the right shots. I suspect he knew at the time that she was coming down with distemper, but hoped he could forestall it. His pills and our earnest administration of them didn't seem to help, and Quartsy just got sicker and sicker. Meanwhile Butch got a weeklong job out of state—we needed the work and the money, and he had to go.

Early one morning, then, I found myself with a dying dog, three young and passionately interested children, and no backup. Quartsy began to have convulsions, and I finally locked her in the bathroom, afraid that in her spasms she might bite someone. Finally she quieted down. I looked timorously at her and went into the bedroom and told the children that Quartsy had died and that now it was time for all of us to go to bed (which it was—

and late too). I kept thinking I had to keep life moving along in as ordinary a routine as possible.

The children were all of them cheerful and very excited. They carefully inspected what they could see of Quartsy—she was lying covered by a towel on the bathroom floor—then brushed their teeth, put on their pajamas, and went to bed. I read a story and sang each one a song. There was only one variation in the usual routine: Naomi (then six years old) bounced into bed, pulled up the covers, and said that she wanted everybody's animals to sleep with. I said incredulously, "What?" She repeated her announcement (it wasn't a request), and then I saw that the other two, Corey (then seven and a half) and Nick (then five years old), were picking up their own every-night-clutched-to-the-bosom stuffed animals, four or five each, and taking them over to their sister without any signs of reluctance, as though it were a standard part of the nightly routine. She went to sleep that night under a small mountain of stuffed toys. Nobody else had any at all, and nobody seemed to mind.

During the night I was woken up by Corey, who said that she had been having bad dreams about how I had died. My husband was away and I didn't feel all that good myself, so I took her in the big bed and we slept together soundly the rest of the night through. There was no word at all from the youngest child.

Next day was a school day. I spent a good deal of time wondering what should I do now: get somebody to come and disappear the dog while the children were away, wait till they got home to do it, or what? Finally, I decided that fate had brought it about that this was the time for us as a family to learn about death—in its proper context, when it actually had happened. So when the children came home after school, I announced that we would be having a funeral. We were going to bury Quartsy on the hill behind our house (where I had already dug a shallow grave in a place where we could go and visit her), and we should pick some flowers and think of nice things to say to each other about what a fine dog she was.

The ceremony went off without a hitch. We made a straggly procession up the hill, me carrying Quartsy and using the bathroom towel as a shroud. We each threw a handful of dirt on her as she lay in the hole, and after I had filled in with the shovel we patted it all down and sprinkled the flowers over her. The children were thrilled and happily proposed that we go down and make a picnic for supper and come back and eat it at the graveside, but by this time I had about had it. I was myself grieved over the dog, and frankly I was beginning to wonder if our three charming children were some kind of undiscovered monsters. Nobody had seemed the least bit sad at any time during the entire episode, just extremely interested and somewhat overstimulated. The idea of a merry picnic at the grave simply revolted me. I said absolutely not, and we all trailed back down the hill.

I can't remember anymore if the former night's procedure with the animals was repeated. I rather think they were left in whoever's bed they were in at bedtime. Corey again had worrisome dreams about my survival and again we slept together, except that I didn't sleep very well this time.

The next morning—a Saturday—Nick appeared, all dressed, shiny, and cheerful. He ate a hearty breakfast and then said, "Hey, Ma, sing me a dead song." Previously he had made no comment whatever about the dog or the funeral or any of the adventures we had been having; he had just come along serenely for the ride, so to say, watching what was going on.

I said, "I don't want to sing a dead song" (I hadn't even had my coffee yet). But my son simply announced his needs and repeated the news bulletin indefinitely. After ten or twenty more requests of "C'mon, Ma, sing me a dead song" my irritation boiled over. I said, "Look, I just don't *feel* like singing a dead song right now. I don't *want* to sing a dead song. If you want a dead song, go sing one yourself." He finally wandered outside.

I drank my coffee and felt abused and neglected. After a while I heard a young voice singing abstractedly out on the back patio, accompanied only by the rolling wheels of a truck he was pushing:

> Go tell Aunt Nancy, go tell Aunt Nancy
> Go tell Aunt Nancy that old Quartsy's dead
>
> The one she's been saving, and saving, and saving
> The one she's been saving to make a feather bed
>
> She died last Friday, she died last Friday
> She died last Friday with an aching in her head . . .

I have to admit my reaction was: well, thank goodness he's thought one up. As the day went on, so did our usual life. We went on our weekly Saturday expedition to the market and the public library. None of the children brought up the subject of the dog or the funeral. Basically, life resumed its old pace and pattern, except that in the following weeks I began to notice Nick was singing quite a large number of dead songs. It got kind of overwhelming. He sang,

Hush, little baby, don't you cry
You know old Quartsy's bound to die
All my trials, Lord, soon be over

He sang,

Who killed old Quartsy? Who killed old Quartsy?
I said the sparrow with my little bow and arrow
It was I, oh it was I

Who dug his grave? Who dug his grave?
I said the snake with my little spade and rake
It was I, oh it was I

He sang,

Old Quartsy is dead and laid in the ground
Laid in the ground, laid in the ground
Old Quartsy is dead and laid in the ground
Way high up

And he sang,

Quartsy died on Sunday, on Sunday, on Sunday
Quartsy died on Sunday when the weather was good
We buried her on Sunday, on Sunday, on Sunday
We buried her on Sunday when the weather was good

And he sang,

I had an old dog and his name was Quartsy
I bet you five dollars he's a good dog too
Come on Quartsy, you good dog you
Come on Quartsy, you good dog you

When Quartsy died, he died so hard
That he shook the ground in my back yard . . .

It seemed to be just endless. I began to worry after a while. For heaven's sake, how many dead songs was he going to come up with? Admittedly his poetic standards were not terribly refined. He just substituted the dog's name for any deceased person or thing mentioned in a song, regardless of rhyme or meter or even sense, and sang on away. How many songs about death did he know, anyway? I had had absolutely no idea of the extent of his repertory of songs about morbidity. I got kind of embarrassed. Admittedly

I had sung all those songs around the place, but I wasn't teaching them to the children, I was just singing what came into my head. (And there are lots of traditional and nontraditional songs about death, if you stop and think about it.)

I thought a lot about the whole episode. For one thing, I was particularly struck by the way that the three different children had chosen to deal with the dog's passing. The older child had taken the possibility of death and laid it on me, I suspect to shield herself from the even more terrifying notion that she herself could die. The six-year-old had found a different solution by calling on all the available animals to protect her, in return, I suppose, for giving them a sociable and comfortable warm bed to sleep in (a very fair arrangement, I thought).

Putting it another way: the older child had expressed her fears through another person, the second through things that she could handle and manipulate, and the third had tried to deal with the desperately un-understandable event symbolically, through language. I began to realize that, of the three, my young son had had the least practice in talking about something so unfamiliar and bizarre as death, and that's probably why he didn't ever say anything much. The girls had chattered on a good bit, but they were older and could read and he didn't know the proper technical terms. The songs allowed him to talk about dying and death and funerals in an appropriate and dignified way.

As he sang on and on and on (quite cheerfully, by the way—there was no tragic note in his dead songs as far as I could tell) I wondered if he wasn't also subliminally absorbing the truly vital message that experience as well as great literature tells us about death: that it comes to everybody and everything—to gray geese and mamas and Cock Robins and Old Rogers and Old Blues, and to Quartsys, too. I gradually began to feel less peculiar about my children knowing all these funny old-timey songs. Maybe they formed a kind of reference library to be called upon when needed?

That's pretty much the way everyone's traditional repertory of folklore works: it just sits there and waits until you want to use it. That's how my son's dead songs worked. He didn't, I suspect, know they were about death until he needed them and called on them in that context. And by gum, checking back through his mental file cabinet, there they were, ready to be called for.

It's only relatively recently that adults began to write special songs for children. Children didn't use to have a special repertoire all for themselves;

they just picked up whatever songs they heard the grown-ups singing and tucked them away for future inspection, whether they fully comprehended them or not. As parents and as teachers and as people who simply exist along with our young on the same planet, it's crucial for us to see to it that our children have available to them the best we have ourselves learned— structurally, poetically, ethically, in all kinds of ways. These patterns and ideas are often absorbed before they are ever obviously needed or ever obviously taught or even understood. It is all the more critical, then, that they be patterns and ideas that are sufficiently flexible and strong that our children can grow within them.

It was around this time that tragedy hit us out of the blue. Naomi climbed on a chair near our small electric cooking stove in our small kitchen. She was in flames before I could reach her from the bedroom. (The dress was manufactured, I believe, before the children's nonflammable clothes laws were enacted. It almost exploded on her.)

Though severely burned, Naomi survived and later even thrived, but like all such major events it had a lasting effect both on her and on her family. We decided to move into Santa Monica, closer to the hospital where Naomi was being treated and where she would eventually undergo many skin grafts and other plastic surgeries. (I have forgotten how many now; they went on literally for years, almost through high school.) We sold the Topanga house and rented a larger but somewhat rickety place near the Santa Monica downtown area, and the children—including Naomi when she was out of the hospital—attended a local elementary school. I kept teaching and Butch kept trying for (and getting some) paying work, and eventually things settled back into as normal as they could be.

One morning, I arrived at St. John's Hospital for a visit with Naomi to be told I should also see a particular social worker in the hospital business office. I had expected that. We had told the admitting officer that we would make monthly payments for the rest of our lives when we first took her to St. John's, but outside of filling in numerous forms concerning our financial condition, the matter hadn't ever been touched on again. I went in to see this lady, and she said, "I want you to know, Mrs. Hawes, that we have arranged for Naomi's medical care to be provided without cost to you under the California act that covers all children faced with catastrophic medical conditions. You may not have heard of it—it passed some years ago as part of the governor's social legislation. We are, of course, happy that you want to contribute some part of these necessary expenses; but I want to tell you that the State of California believes that your most important repayment would be the rearing of all your three children into three responsible, well-educated, productive citizens. If your son or your other daughter is taking music lessons, for instance, do not cancel them in order to pay those few dollars to the state. These funds are to take proper care of your injured daughter, in order that you and your husband can continue to take care of your entire family."

I have never forgotten that meeting. It was my first taste of what these days would be called socialized medicine. I took it very seriously and I liked it.

⌒⌒

Even back in the Topanga days, Butch and I had decided I had better try to revive my old Cambridge teaching career. I had set about to work up some classes and started at UCLA's University Extension. The director had once met my sister at some kind of summer picnic and said she sang the most beautiful songs he had ever heard. Apparently he never forgot them, for when I got in touch with him (at Shirley's suggestion) he thought my idea of teaching courses for adults on how to accompany folksongs was well worth trying.

I started out on a Tuesday evening with one class in UCLA's music hall, and then the whole enterprise just zoomed. Apparently, we had begun at exactly the right moment of the folk music revival in Los Angeles, for after that I received invitations from several local state universities, as well as from community organizations. Added to my own private classes, which had increased both in size and number, I wound up teaching all there was possibly time for: every weeknight, and occasionally Saturday and Sunday afternoons. Eventually there were those who muttered that if matters continued like this, I would wind up leading "Down in the Valley" in the Hollywood Bowl—with each audience member outfitted with guitar and song sheet.

A large part of my success, as I've already said, was that I happened to start at the right time, but some of it I believe was due to the quality of songs that I taught. I never taught a song that I was not prepared to repeat several hundred times with real emotion, and people always respond to that, especially when they can hear themselves contributing to the musicality and the true impact of the song. As a group we always wound up sounding good, and we didn't stop until we were at least on the verge of that. And then I knew enough about the songs and the people who sang them to give the students some idea of what lay behind even the most prosaic musical number, and I learned how to tell stories that brought them all alive. Finally, and probably least important, I became able to sneak in just enough music theory to enable all students to transpose relatively easily and fit in with other players in different keys. Poor things, most had been brainwashed by the educational system to believe that music literacy was both essential to making music and extremely difficult to learn. But neither of these things was really true; I took them right up to the edge of music literacy before they even knew it.

(A remarkable Irish flute player told me many years later that his father had insisted that he learn note reading, and so he always taught it to his own students now. "It comes in so handy," he confided, "for starting the tunes." I agreed.)

My classes gradually came to conform roughly with the academic year and, in due course, announced themselves as beginning, intermediate, and advanced. But the structure of each session, regardless of level, was always the same: each introduced two new songs (one easy—two chords only—and one more musically complex) and one new instrumental technique (a new key, bass runs in C, arpeggios, walking bass). Somewhere there was a brief discussion of the musical elements involved, perhaps some vocal harmony techniques and ideas, along with a thorough review of earlier work and resinging of old favorites.

During the summer months I broke the pattern and scheduled a weekly repertoire class, open to all levels of experience on any suitable instrument. Participants would come in and pass by my open guitar case lying by the front door into which they would contribute two or three dollars for the evening, for which they would receive song sheets containing four new songs, one of which was always accessible to two-chord beginners and another of which called for some interesting singing (for example, a round or a church hymn). Mother's insistence, over all my objections, on my learning touch typing at the age of nine, along with all the many years of practice since, meant I could produce twenty to thirty song sheets using flimsy paper and carbons with only five retypings. I didn't allow tape recordings to be made during class because the machines of that day required plugging into the wall and I hated having to climb over all those snaky wires while I was teaching. Every now and again, though, I would announce a general taping session, where I would sing a verse or two of each song we had learned so far to a forest of recorders to help everyone keep the tunes in mind.

All in all, these repertoire classes, as I called them, were the most fun of anything, and that gave me something to think about when I began changing my overall curricula. In the meantime, teaching at state colleges was giving me new perspectives on what I could or should or might be doing. Generally I was approached by the various music departments, who were much more interested in the folksong repertoire than the guitar. Music students began to be joined by numerous other undergraduates preparing for careers in elementary education, and then there were strays from the summer repertoire classes who kept talking about what fun they were. I began to think about preparing a course in American/European folksongs without instruments, and that, of course, demanded rethinking to put it within a then-acceptable academic context.

I tried out several experiments with the content of my courses and found that teaching was getting exciting again. Not only music, but anthropology and folklore college departments seemed to like what I was doing, especially at what is now known as California State University at Northridge (CSUN)—until 1972 called San Fernando Valley State College (SFV)—where a brilliant anthropologist was developing an experimental curriculum for the teaching of undergraduate anthropology based on examinations of and experiences with the art forms of all societies. His name was Dr. Edmund Carpenter, and we worked together very happily for some years until he left the campus after an unseemly and bitter quarrel with the administration.

I learned an incredible amount from Ted (as most people called him), foremost of all to take pleasure and strength from my unusual background and not to worry so much about my lack of standard academic preparation. He urged me strongly to begin to teach folklore courses as well as folk music courses on his campus. When I said I didn't know the literature well enough, he replied as I suspect my mother would have (though without using the Latin). From his standpoint I knew the essence of the field well, if in a different and important way. The rest was just a question of filling in the blank spots, and for that, "By doing, you learn to do."

And as I did, gradually my resolve stiffened and I found myself teaching full time in an academic position in the anthropology department of San Fernando State. I taught Introductory Folklore, American Folk Music, Introductory Ethnomusicology, and Field Study Folklore. I sort of relaxed in some ways, and without the pressure my intellectual development began blooming again. I began to develop my own ideas, ideas that I would later develop into academically respectable papers and articles.

I remember hours sitting in the campus café with my best friends and colleagues—such exciting people as Councill Taylor, Joan Rayfield, Fred Katz—and just glorying in the conversation. There had been nothing like it in my experience before: engaging with fellow professionals who understood what I was trying to do because they were engaged in similar intellectual ventures. For the first time in my life, it seemed to me, I had real colleagues to work with.

I came home late one evening after a full day's teaching to discover the entire family sound asleep and the following "Butch Hawes Special" lying on the kitchen table:

> Oh I wish I had a colleague I could call my own
> Instead of all these routine friends I has
> For the whole world knows, as friendship goes
> Interaction with a colleague's got a lot more class . . .

I could always count on my husband not to let me get too big for my britches.

EIGHT

College Teaching

One of my earliest teaching problems, especially obvious in this new formal college setting, turned out to be definitional. This was a new concern for me. In guitar classes I could say, "Well, let's see how it sounds," and away we would go, leaving all inscrutable little intellectual questions far behind. But I couldn't be so cavalier in Introductory Folklore, Ethnomusicology, or American Folk Music; I had to make a reasonable attempt to see to it that everybody had a reasonable understanding of what I was talking about.

And it quickly turned out that almost everyone had a different and highly simplified idea of what the course content actually was. In Introductory Folklore, for instance, one student would be thinking in terms of world mythology; another of anything sung by the Kingston Trio or Pete Seeger; yet another of Grimm's fairy tales, or other people's untrue ideas (which always turned out to be "superstitions"). I found myself spending the first half of each semester broadening the class's concept of the field, and the last half narrowing it back down from their happy attempts to include all behavior and communication under folklore.

In American Folk Music, likewise, I kept trying to state my definition of the field more clearly, while thinking always it would be so much easier if I had stronger examples to present. My own repertoire of "folksongs"—

"Down in the Valley," "Go Tell Aunt Nancy," "Careless Love"—were generally pieces of exotica to young Californians. At last one day, the "Happy Birthday" song popped into my head and I could hear the contented clicking of pieces falling into place. "Oh, so *that's* what she means!" exuded from every happily settled mind in the room. That song had all the qualifications I had been outlining. It had not been taught, but every single person knew it; many students knew variations; no one could remember having consciously learned it, and so on. Drawing courage from this, we went straight on to "For She's a Jolly Good Fellow" and we were past the first major hurdle.

Actually, I was myself off and running too, but in a slightly different direction. The thing that has always interested me about musical folklore (and nonmusical folklore as well) is: why is it always with us anyway? To put this in terms of the repertoire I was dealing with, why does the rather elementary "Happy Birthday" song remain carved into the brain cells of every person who hears it once only (and gets no prize for learning it), when there are so many more interesting things she might prefer to remember? Why did almost every student in class know the rhyme "Starlight, star bright / first star I see tonight / I wish I may, I wish I might / have the wish I wish tonight"? I have spent much of my adult life worrying over just such, to me, fascinating questions.

I truly believe that such scraps of formulaic knowledge contain in them both comforting and discomforting statements concerning the deepest beliefs and ways of a culture. My brother's highly developed research into communication systems (Cantometrics, Choreometrics, et al.) uses a very large frame for such considerations, and occasionally he and I crossed into each other's territory. One day, for instance, I was driving to work along the Santa Monica freeway wondering idly why the Jefferson Airplane (an early rock band) played so terribly loud. I had heard them just a while before and they nearly took the top of my head off. I had been told—in what is probably coming to be a local legend—that a small dog had once wandered into the auditorium where they were rehearsing and had fallen over dead in a few minutes.

As I wondered, two images kept coming into my mind: the Jefferson Airplane's electric bass player, a willowy, fragile-looking fellow who played his auditorium-shaking notes with a totally relaxed hand (looking, as I remember, far away); and the famous picture of Louis Armstrong, face contorted with sweat, blowing his brains out into his New Orleans jazz trumpet but, with all his passion and commitment, not producing half the decibels of the bass player. Everything I thought I had understood seemed turned upside down all of a sudden.

I decided perhaps the whole phenomenon might have something to do with "cool," a term that was then just coming into fashion. The player who made the *most* noise was exerting the *least* human energy and vice versa. This seemed physiologically backwards, but I realized, on exploring the idea further, that when I drove the freeway I was behaving in just the same reversed fashion. As I drove, only pressing my foot lightly and turning the wheel gently, I was traveling at an infinitely faster speed than I could have gone on foot, exerting every bit of human physical energy I had available. So, perhaps the idea of "cool" had an inverse relationship with the idea of general impact or power. The less energy you put out, the more control you have (the ultimate example, perhaps, being the delicate pressing of the final button that must precede an atomic blast).

I wasn't sure I liked my tentative conclusion, but it was fun trying to think that way—of course not only my brother, but pioneers like Marshall McLuhan and Ted Carpenter were already miles ahead of me—and to use that kind of investigatory technique on the material I was teaching. Since I had found that students really seemed to identify with "Happy Birthday to You" and the aligned traditions (cake cutting, blowing out the candles, and so on) I had started out with, I decided to use children's folklore for the subject of my first several weeks of lectures, pulling as much out of the class members as I could in terms of the examination of their own personal recollections. After all, everybody has been a child. And since children's folklore is remarkably stable (often over centuries), remarkably flexible (easy to alter and bring "up to date"), and remarkably close to the bone (full of emotional content, if one can just pull back and look at it), the general topic of childlore made for a really involving course opening.

I would often start out with the wonderful statement I had read somewhere: "If there were a rope stretched across the country from San Diego, California, to Portland, Maine, all the children jumping along that rope would be jumping to the same rhymes." Students liked to think of which ones, sometimes looking them up in my own files of jump rope rhymes, leading them willy-nilly into regional collections and even journal research.

The creative and kindly Dr. Herbert Halpert, at a national meeting of the American Folklore Society, had once suggested that childlore might be a fruitful path for me, and I found it so engaging that it became my own personal research area for many years. As a teaching vehicle it managed nicely to include both spoken words (rhymes, stories) and music. Although I taught separate courses on folklore and on American music, the processes behind the two were always the same to me, and childlore brought this out immediately. And then I already had such wonderful observational possibilities at home, with three children and their friends living their lives right under my maternal nose. Generally, the topic allowed me to meld my life with my teaching.

One day, while I was washing dishes, I saw my oldest daughter, at the age of eight or nine, bouncing a ball on the patio behind the house. Apparently she had decided on her own to get entirely through the traditional game "A, my name is (Alice) and my husband's name is (Andrew) and I come from (Arizona) and I sell (apples). B, my name is (Barry) . . ." without error. This is arguably one of the most difficult tasks I can think of. Not only do you have to keep the ball bouncing in rhythm and without pause, but you have to come in with the proper wording exactly on the beat—and if you make any mistake, you have to start all over again from the beginning. I thought, as I watched her, of an article I had read that said that parents and teachers should realize that children up to the age of maturity have a low attention span, and their work should be assigned with that in mind. The authors should have seen Corey as she—with no one watching that she knew of—went on and on in her self-imposed task. I began to get a bit desperate as the time dragged by and she started all over yet another time. I did not want to interrupt this truly Herculean endeavor, and she went on and on doggedly until at last the sky began to darken and I could legitimately call her in for supper.

We never discussed the episode and I do not know if she ever reached her improbable goal, but this and other episodes turned my attention from the rhymes of play alone to the associated behaviors as well. I would urge my students to pay attention to what was going on in the general surround, as well as to any folkloric texts, and they turned in many interesting short case studies that augmented my own. Eventually I turned my own and my students' observations into an academic paper entitled "Law and Order on the Playground" that was printed in *Games in Education and Development*, edited by Lloyda M. Shears and Eli M. Bower. An abridged version appears just below.

The final bell of the day rang as I was passing a Santa Monica elementary school one spring afternoon, and the children began to pour out of the play yard. Two little girls, aged perhaps eight or nine, walked past me deep in conversation.

"Let's play step on a crack, break your mother's back!" "Naw, let's play monkey faces. That's lots better. See, the good thing about monkey faces is you can step on all the cracks! You can stomp the cracks, if you want to, or you can wipe your feet all over the cracks. The only thing is, you can't step on a square that has a monkey face on it."

Apparently a "monkey face" was the contractor's symbol imprinted on the sidewalk cement, for I watched them walk away, stepping boldly on all the cracks they passed and taking big running leaps over the tabooed section of pavement.

As I watched the two little girls, it seemed plain that a large part of the pleasure they found in the activity stemmed from their realization that they were doing more than playing "monkey faces," they were also not playing "step on a crack, break your mother's back." Their particular emotional gratification hinged upon their knowledge of both games, not just the one they elected to play. Were there two games here? Or was one simply a reverse image of the other, or perhaps a permissible variation in the rules?

Folklorists tend to pose this kind of problem in terms of the twin factors of stability and variation in traditional forms. When dealing with children's traditional materials, one is almost always confronted by both dimensions stretched to their utmost. The historical continuity of childlore is one of the most remarkable aspects of the human condition. Revolutions, wars, vast migrations often seem to have had little or no effect upon the private world of the children involved. Some of the counting-out rhymes still chanted on modern-day playgrounds can be traced to Celtic languages spoken by Britons in pre-Roman times. Spanish children in the New World still play the singing games that their Old World cousins play, although an ocean and a two-hundred-year time span lie between. Marbles, kites, cat's cradle, and hop-scotch go back before recorded human history, and as a child in Texas I used to thump on my brother's back in a guessing game mentioned by Petronius.

At the same time, variation is apparently as essential as stability. One of the perplexing difficulties encountered in dealing with children's lore is that out of a hundred renditions of the "same" counting-out rhyme, for example, almost no two will be exactly identical. And when adult intervention, print, and other stabilizing forces enter into the picture, as in the case of the nursery or "Mother Goose" rhymes, then the parodies begin:

> Hickory dickory dock, two mice ran up the clock
> The clock struck one, and the other one got away
> [or]
> Hickory dickory dock, two mice ran up the clock
> The clock struck one, the other escaped with minor injuries
>   (etc. ad infinitum)

The pleasure intrinsic to parody—which is only a kind of variation after all—seems to lie in a sort of double vision. One must know the original in order to savor the adventuresomeness of the variation, and thus, to some extent, both are reinforced. In this sense, it seems quite possible that only those cultural items that are susceptible to variation have much of a chance at long-term survival, and this may in part account for the longevity of the child's own tradition in which variation flourishes.

The apparently paradoxical coexistence of rules and innovation (or, in other terms, stability and variation) may be further explored by looking at those play activities sometimes referred to as "games of individual skill," such as jacks, ball bouncing, and hop-scotch. Those games parallel the jokes, nonsense rhymes, and tongue twisters of childlore in at least two dimensions: they circulate primarily among the seven-to-twelve-year-old peer group, and they are generally learned informally, by watching and listening to other children at play.

Most of the games of individual skill are extremely tightly structured. To take jacks as an example, each player in turn must maneuver through a lengthy sequence of highly restricted movements or subgames, any variation in which requires the player to give up his turn to the next player. In actual play, however, in spite of the large number of requirements on which agreement is general—a player may not move any jack except the one in play, all jacks must be picked up first one at a time, then two at a time, and so on—there are also a large number of variables that are free-floating, open to discussion, and may be placed in or left out of the round of play being planned.

The order in which the various moves, or subgames, are made is a case in point. Most children start with "Babies" or "Plainsies," in which each jack is simply picked up without additional flourishes, but after the first round any or all of the following moves may be required: Pigs in the pen; Eggs in the basket; Upsies; Downsies; Around the world; Rolling down Broadway; Shooting stars; and so on for fifty or so variations.

Once the sequence has been agreed upon, there are still a number of points of play that are open to a number of kinds of settlement. What is to be done, for example, about "kissies" (two jacks that land touching each other) or "haystacks" (one jack on top of another)? Can you play "cart before the horse," in which a player working on her "foursies" is allowed to pick up the ten jacks in the order two-four-four, rather than four-four-two?

The significant point is that agreement on all these questions is only temporary; all such rules are considered to be in effect only for the duration of the particular play session about to begin. Although children who often play together may evolve a mutually acceptable routine, should one or another grow bored with the arrangement, it is these points that would be open to negotiation and not the "regular" rules.

Essentially, then, the traditional rules for playing jacks are constructed to include a variation factor, which is itself an actual part of the rules, and which, through millions of rounds of play, has successfully resisted all the powerful forces of stabilization. In games where the rules have been officially stabilized by adult invention or decree—most prominently tetherball, handball, and four square—children have countered by inventing their own self-imposed areas of variation.

In many public schools nowadays, traditional games such as jacks, jump rope, marbles, and the like have either been forbidden outright or are strongly discouraged. Official explanations vary, but the general impression emerges that teachers consider that the traditional games lead to "fighting," that they are disorderly and hard to police. Schoolchildren are instead encouraged, and in some cases required, to play officially approved games for which there are rules and rulebooks that may be consulted.

On several California elementary schoolyards, however, children almost always, before playing rulebook handball, "tap" that a number of defined variations be out or fair:

"Fifty-fifties" or "pop-ups": ball hits at junction of wall
and ground
"Dead killers": ball rolls back, preventing further play
"Babies": a low soft hit

And so forth through a list of perhaps twenty permutations. Further, play can be "locked out" by allowing no more players into the game; a "tea party" can be held, allowing only two players to participate at a time; or the call can go up for "pink elephants," where some players line up against the wall and attempt to avoid being hit on the bounce by others. Very few teachers appear to be aware that the children are playing by their own rules, but the folklore files at California State University at Northridge are full of such examples; similar principles are often applied to other officially sanctioned games.

So, in the lifestyle of the American playground, there appears to be a kind of fundamental need for a bifurcated game structure: one axis consisting of the unchangeable rules, the other of those aspects of the game that are subject to variation. This, then, suggests that the games "step on a crack, break your mother's back" and "monkey faces" are indeed two aspects of the same thing. "Step on a crack" has only one rule, so to speak, so that a built-in variation factor is impossible; hence the need to invent a reversal or parody. The existence of the "two" games may then allow the players the same leeway for attaining temporary consensus that the variation factor permits in other traditional games.

For it is critical to remember that the agreement is only temporary; it must be affirmed and reaffirmed each time play begins via a preplay discussion, which may be both prolonged and vociferous. Indeed, even after play is under way, its course may be changed by the shout of "I tap . . ." or "Dibs on . . ." The interjection of these magical formulas requires immediate readjustment on the part of all the players; lacking this, the entire group shatters into passionate splinter units, the better to debate the issue. Not infrequently it can be observed that a group will use the entire time available for play in a bitter—but apparently refreshing—discussion over the "rules." No one seems to mind, really, that the game never gets played.

No wonder the decibel rate of our schoolyards is so high: floating over our playgrounds are the shrill, intense voices of a thousand decision makers at work—testing, probing, rearranging, counterposing—all very exhausting and unnecessary in the tidier-minded adult world. But one of my students pointed out that a particular series of "I taps" invariably accompanied the entrance into a handball game of a remarkably tall child; apparently the game was improved for all by a bit of temporary group editing. What is going on here really?

Variation is frequently productive of uproar—there is absolutely no doubt about that. However, it can also promote flexibility and the knack of achieving compromise. Our children appear to have taken their cultural stance; they will cheerfully risk chaos any day in order to preserve a satisfactory degree of group and individual autonomy. And theirs is a more structurally complex position than may first appear, for by the time the children have reached the game-playing age, they have, by definition, learned that there are some immutables, some rules that cannot be challenged or there is no game at all. It is the area in which change is possible that interests them most, and quite properly so.

It is, after all, possible that the children are right for the needs of their culture—that in terms of the democratic way of life, it is far more important for them to practice reaching and working within a temporary consensus than to learn obedience to an unchanging set of requirements. And so, from the perspective of the playground, "law-and-order" appears not as a static, monolithic single unit, but as "law" and "order," twin channels through which the human control of the human destiny may flow. And it seems that we should try to comprehend these processes better before we so casually, and so ineffectually, attempt to interfere by administrative fiat, invention, or codification. As adults, we stand to learn much, for our children, as they play, are themselves grappling with an issue of central importance to a democratic society such as ours: the interlock of order and flexibility, group consensus and individual freedom, stability and change.

So far I have not given enough credit or coverage to the critically important role my students were playing in all my writing, thinking, and intellectual discoveries. Not only had they stimulated my investigation of children's lore, they had provided me with bushels and bushels of data, that critical substance that is essential to folklore studies. I had assured the availability of ever more of this raw information by requiring each student in a folklore or folk music class to turn in a collection project that had been amassed through talking with or directly observing other human beings. And it was their contributions that made my previously cited discussions possible.

I made this requirement imperative for all students because I deeply believed in its academic importance: they learned so much from it. They were at complete liberty to develop their own projects as they preferred or as the projects they had chosen made inevitable. I did strongly recommend that for their first venture into live collecting they consider one of three alternatives: using themselves as "informants" (pointing out that they would be the most cooperative and easily available subjects they would ever find), using their friends or family members as sources, or observing groups engaged in some variety of normally public activity—playground games, for example. All data had to be presented along with any immediately available background information or a description of the context. I seriously discouraged using a first collecting experience to tackle an unfamiliar ethnicity or neighborhood, suggesting that working with even an exchange student might raise additional analytical problems they were not yet aware of.

For yet another part of the assignment was to demonstrate that they had put some recognizable thought into the project. I urged them not to try to figure out "what it all means," pointing out that the way they chose to organize the presentation of the raw data would itself disclose some part at least of their thinking—if they reported it in historical or geographic terms or as a personal history. At all times they were to bear in mind that they were dealing with part of the contents of another person's head; that was very different from sociological or economic data (not better or worse, just different) and therefore their responsibilities became different. I sometimes told them of a former student who had said to me at the end of a semester, "Mrs. Hawes, you taught me all about how to collect. What you didn't teach me was how to *stop* collecting. I collected hiccup cures from this old lady next door, and now every single time I come home she's out on her front porch telling me that she just remembered another one. I've gotten so I sneak in by the alley just to avoid her. I just can't get her to understand that I already turned in my paper." I told him that I was sorry; he had gotten a good grade and now he had to start paying for it. He had made this lady feel that she knew important things, and she would never again think differently. "You didn't find an informant," I told him, "you made a friend. And now you have to take care of this friend's feelings."

I tried to be both sensitive and helpful to my students' position, and I gradually began sending an appreciative letter to individual "informants" who had themselves obviously thought hard about their interviews. I thanked them for their contribution to the college folklore archive—even though it did not actually exist at the time—and I wrote each letter separately on the formal embossed university stationery. To my surprise, quite a few students later told me that my letters had later appeared, framed and hung prominently, on their addressee's living room walls.

Collections were handed back before the end of the semester, with my pencil comments and requests for more information scribbled in the margins. The students were asked to return their amplified collections to me *only* if they wanted them to be in the college folklore collection (with names blanked out where important). Most of them did, and most of them worked very hard on their projects. Some even began to feel at least some of the emotional heat of their data.

Late one afternoon I was sitting in my office, getting up the energy to go home, when a student from one of my folklore classes came in, almost threw a blue folder on my desk, and said, "I know it's late and it isn't as good as I wanted it to be, but when I work on it I get to crying and I just can't stand to fool with it any more." I found out later that she was a social worker and counselor at a prison for female juvenile delinquents in downtown Los Angeles. At the time, I just tried to calm her down, pointing out that it was exam week and she wasn't that late anyway. I assured her I would read her paper right away and recommended that she should go home and get some sleep. She had titled her paper "La Llorona in Juvenile Hall."

Naturally, I read it as soon as I got home. Her data consisted of some fifty or so brief items that folklorists might call superstitions, rudimentary legends, or traditional statements of belief. They were all quite short, some hardly more than a sentence, and all centered upon a dangerous female ghost sometimes referred to as La Llorona (a widespread Mexican spectral figure, possibly of early European origin and almost always described as a mother vainly searching for her children whom she had lost or murdered). I recognized her immediately, but at the time I felt a bit disappointed that she was presented with so little emotional or poetic detail. These were plain, factual statements, most of them beginning "There is a woman who . . . ." But the more I read them, the more I began to understand why my student had found them so emotionally draining. Collectively, they had an unexpectedly strong impact.

During the next months, I spoke with my student several times, urging her to develop her paper further, but she was adamant: she just didn't want to think about it any more. I finally put it away, but it kept on coming back into my mind. Several years later, I located her and asked permission to try working up a study of her data myself. I also titled it "La Llorona in Juvenile Hall," and in 1968 it was published in *Western Folklore*, the journal of the California Folklore Society. It was my first shot at an academic paper and I now find it a bit stuffy and overdetailed, but I had performed an interesting exercise in it: I had taken all the possible methods of textual analysis I could find and used each to work through all the data provided in hopes that, all together, they might point me toward a truly defensible final argument. To my surprise, the most powerful turned out to be Vladimir Propp's structural analytic system of the folk tale, since it focused me finally on the incompleteness of almost every single fragmentary bit of data I had: all the statements recorded had the beginnings of a tale, but almost none had endings. It seemed to me they deeply reflected exactly what was going on in the lives of these tellers and just why and how they had stripped their statements to the brutal facts alone. As such they were not "mere superstitious beliefs" (as some of the collector's supervisors put it), but carefully worded reflections of the real state of affairs for the residents of Juvenile Hall. Maybe, I wondered, that could be true of all ghosts; maybe the ghost figure everywhere was a concluding reflection of unfilled longings, incomplete lives, unkept promises.

I was a bit disappointed in the lack of enthusiasm with which this general hypothesis was received by many folklorists, but I later decided it had been perhaps simply outshone by the widespread interest in the history and provenance of the La Llorona figure herself. It also reflected how little academic or scholarly attention was being paid at that time to the enormous mine of information available within the Mexican and Mexican American traditional tale repertoires.

I had rather hoped some similar project might attract a young Hispanic scholar in a folklore class, but it never happened. A year or so later, a young Mexican American woman did hand in a collection that included a *corrido* (a storytelling song), which a member of her extended family had composed immediately after the collapse of the San Francisquito Dam. This tragedy had occurred in 1928. Several local Valley towns were severely damaged and casualties were high, at least equaling the better-known San Francisco earthquake and fire of twenty-two years before. My student had taped, transcribed, and translated the many verses of this family-preserved local corrido and told how it came to be written, but she later proved unwilling to put it into a publishable format. It is not unusual for a kind of fog to arise between local singers and the traditional songs they have learned—perhaps old-fashioned creations seem just too ordinary and even a bit embarrassing. So with the collector's permission, I later wrote up the song myself, pointing out the accuracy and delicacy of the narrative poetry and how well its unschooled farmer/composer had understood and utilized the classic corrido form. The article was published in *Western Folklore* in 1974.

An old friend, Sandy Ives, the folklorist, especially liked the ending of "El Corrido de la Inundacion de la Presa de San Francisquito: The Story of a Local Ballad," and did me the honor of quoting my last paragraphs in some of his talks:

> "El Corrido de la Inundacion de la Presa de San Francisquito" is not, in terms of conventional criteria, an important song, certainly not a "big" song. There is no evidence that anyone other than Sr. Encinas (its composer) ever sang it, or, indeed, that until he recorded it for his friend, anyone outside the family ever even heard it. It tells only those details of the disaster which were of direct significance to the Encinas family; possibly—even probably—there were other Saint Francis Dam *corridos* by other now unknown *corridistas* that we shall never hear. In a way, this does not matter. Art has always been expendable, and songs, like people, are born and die every day.
>
> But occasionally to examine the "little" songs, the family songs, the songs of clearly local interest, is to bring us close to the ever-marvelous thrust of ordinary men to give dignity and pattern to their life experience. And it may cause us also to look with even greater respect at the subtle structures of the traditional forms through which these expressive voices are channeled to take their place with those of all other peoples.

NINE

Off-Campus Excursions

Through the 1950s and 60s, my university experience was continually extended and salted by work outside the campus with many different kinds of people. Especially during the fifties there was an outburst of public "folk" activities including festivals, concerts, and other special events like the annual Topanga Banjo and Fiddle Contest and such. The University of California at Los Angeles hosted several very important two- and three-day celebrations, as did UC San Diego, but the grandfather of this category was the Berkeley Folk Festival, which eventually featured every important traditional musician in the land from Almeda Riddle to Pete Seeger, from Lightning Hopkins to Joan Baez. It was enormous fun; they always politely included "Bess and Butch Hawes" in the festival's enormous casts and we always brought along our three children (who later attended UC Berkeley at various times and periods), so our family had a truly pleasurable four or five days in Berkeley to look forward to every summer.

And then there was always the Idyllwild Arts Center and its valiant attempt to build a summer arts colony in the beautiful mountains behind Palm Springs. Idyllwild itself was a tiny mountain community reachable only by a precipitous ascent on a somewhat scary highway, and occasionally our noble Jeep under its heavy load seemed to lose heart entirely and simply stopped. We were informed by more experienced commuters that the condition was "vapor lock," due to the sudden gain in altitude. We ourselves were sometimes similarly afflicted. Butch eventually wrote a song in commemoration:

> Oh, I was half a mi-dle from Idyllwi-dle
>   when my motor sprang a vapor locket
> My lungs protruded from the altituded
>   and my ticker went "tick-tock-a-pocket"
> Oh Idyllwi-dle what diddle I do
>   to wind up winded up here in the blue?
> Oh my brain is addled and I'll be so glad-dled
>   just to see sea level again
>
> I'm walking up to the mess hall dragging my feet
>   in the Idyllwi-dle waddle with the winded beat

When you finally achieved the arts center, it turned out to be a pleasant collection of stone structures and open performance spaces run in conjunction with the music department at the University of Southern California. The center had a young people's orchestra, instrumental instruction, art and ceramic studios, a program of evening concerts, and many other pleasant summer activities. For several years, in synthesis with the ongoing folk music revival, it had weeklong folk music programs; and under Sam Hinton's steady and professional guidance a large number of exceptional musicians of the period were there, in a way themselves enjoying their own private revival: exchanging songs, gossip and family news, guitar licks and fiddle tunings, ideas and tall tales, teaching and performing when and as they wanted to. For them, I suspect, it was a once-in-a-lifetime chance to have some time—one week, even two weeks—to breathe deeply and refuel their artistic engines.

As a family we were there, I believe, for three summers in the late 1950s. To give just an impression of how rich the programs were, I recall Almeda Riddle, Jimmy Driftwood, Brownie McGhee, Pete Seeger, the folklorist and singer Roger Abrahams, the Georgia Sea Island Singers, a fine Hawaiian slack key guitarist whose name I can't now recall, and many local musicians—Guy Carawan, Frank Hamilton—and holding it all together everyone's favorite, Sam Hinton.

In the summer of 1964, I was invited by Idyllwild to act as organizer/folklorist for an unusual program (possibly suggested by Sam): a one-week session with the Georgia Sea Island Singers to help Los Angeles schoolteachers learn about African American musical styles. Maybe the program was not as definite as that—I no longer remember—but as I understood it, we were supposed to do something about strengthening West Coast urban city schoolteachers' understanding of the musical background from which most of their pupils had emerged.

I suggested to the Sea Islanders that one of their lead singers, Bessie Jones, should begin to share what I already knew she knew: her own fascinating repertoire of children's game songs. All of the other Sea Island Singers were familiar with them, of course, so we started out, with Bessie being head teacher and the others acting as demonstrators. We had also planned a daily session to teach their venerable spiritual repertoire, but somehow that fell apart. I don't know if I got so fascinated with what Mrs. Jones was doing in her special area that I didn't work enough at presenting the other larger session, or else we all (Singers and class and I) got discouraged at how hard it was going to be to learn these marvelous songs well. I don't know—I suspect there was a bit of both in what happened.

Anyway, the children's games classes were a knockout, sometimes happening twice a day and always full of players. Bessie Jones displayed her invariable mastery of the moment, her unshakable poise, and her unmatchable joy and pleasure in what she was doing as she persuaded the random assemblages of mostly white elementary-school teachers who appeared before her to do things they never had done before. I was myself entranced because I got so much opportunity to watch a master teacher from essentially another culture at work, and I learned an enormous amount. Later, Mrs. Jones and I joined forces to coauthor a book of her children's repertoire titled *Step It Down*. Basically it was her book: her repertory, her ideas. I acted as secretary, transcribing the words and music, organizing the wide range of material she offered, and noting down her comments and thoughts. During the first weeks, I spent every evening transcribing the day's sessions word for word; although I later got less self-demanding, I always found that the process had been extraordinarily productive.

Mrs. Jones was not only a remarkable performer with a repertoire of songs that demonstrated her sensitivity and taste, she was also an intellectual, by which I mean someone who consistently thinks about what she is saying. I have not met many in my life, and very few of them have been traditional artists (who are much more likely to be great gatherers, rememberers, and willing sharers). Mrs. Jones had thought and continued to think about the content of every one of her songs; she puzzled over their inconsistencies and she tried to fit them in coherently to her own philosophy, especially in the area of child training. She was constantly explaining them to everybody, using her own verbal shorthand, and if you weren't quick you missed the meaning she was trying to convey.

In the general introduction to *Step It Down* and also in each chapter heading, I wrote about the education messages Mrs. Jones was continually sending. I placed my remarks there because I didn't want a lot of language to get in the way of the songs and dances themselves, but I think I would not do it that way again. Most people, I believe, never get around to reading introductory material and so probably missed a large part of what Mrs. Jones was trying to convey. At least I know that after that experience I have found myself meticulously reading introductions to any serious book I tackle.

And I had learned what I knew through the rigorous discipline of transcription. For example, it took me at least ten days of word-for-word transcribing until, during a fog of boredom, I wrote down that she had said, "That one is a game. Of course, it's a play too, but really it's a game." And it hit me like a mental firecracker that she had used those words differently right from the beginning. I had thought them synonyms (they were to me), but checking back I realized that she had consistently used one term to indicate the presence of competition and the other for its absence, and she was prescribing the use of one or the other in varying circumstances. I was really excited, and I started being even more careful to listen and transcribe accurately.

After having her as my house guest for a week later on, I began to sort out the educational ideas I had been hearing or watching. Here are a few:

Along with the other Sea Island Singers, she felt that you learned by being encouraged to try and by being complimented for what you were able to do. I almost never heard her criticize an attempt, no matter how clumsy or ill-considered. I found it personally embarrassing when so many of the young female students tried to insert their ideas of "sexy" movements into the much more straightforward traditional dance style, but no Sea Islander ever said a word. Another time, Mrs. Jones was showing me a complicated foot-tapping pattern involving both feet hitting the floor at the same instant every now and then. When I would fail to bring both feet down *exactly* together, she would clap her hands and say, "Ooh, you made a *double beat!*"

One student was having great difficulty keeping her feet flat on the floor, as so many of the shuffling dance steps required. She simply could not keep from assuming a balletic on-the-toes position. She was getting embarrassed by this, and the other students (me included) were inventing little practice moves she could work on in order to keep her heels down and her feet flat on the floor. Mrs. Jones, however, came in one morning and announced with real delight that she had remembered a dance that was *good for* people who couldn't keep their heels down; she then proceeded to teach us the only dance she knew that was done on tip-toes. Mrs. Jones's "good for" was positive; mine was negative. That gave me plenty to think about.

In just one more example of the difficulties and splendors of trying to explain things across cultural lines, the Sea Islanders often accompanied their group singing with clapped polyrhythms as complex as those performed by any jazz drummer or tap dancer. For one thing, they clapped in parts—in tenor, baritone, and bass ranges—making their rhythms unmistakably African-based, rather than the essentially single pitch most common in Scottish or British drum bands. The results of the Sea Island style were tantalizingly difficult to replicate or analyze. During one hand-clapping lesson, I asked Mrs. Jones if she would "start clapping alone first, and then Emma can come in later so I can see how her clapping pattern works against yours." Mrs. Jones took a long time to answer. "Emma don't clap against me," she said, "she claps *with* me." For me, that was a moment of real enlightenment. I realized that when I asked a student to do something with me, I expected a duplication of my own movements. For Mrs. Jones, the claps were so much more. She wanted them to be complementary but different, working out of a conjoined musical impulse.

I only once saw her truly upset with a student, one whose turn had come to be the center figure in a ring play and who strolled from the surrounding ring obviously planning what she was going to do during her turn. Mrs. Jones almost lost it there. "No, no, no!" she cried, "You got to dance it, you got to move with the rhythm, you got to do it right!" And I began to realize that for her "doing it right" was not a question of minor issues such as posture or particular hand or foot positions; it was being with the music and with the other dancers, being a part of something bigger and more unifying. Truly, to me, Mrs. Bessie Jones was a real intellectual and a brilliant, thoughtful, analytical, and generous spirit who tried to make joyful and interesting every day of her life. I still miss her and always will. I hope I can hand on at least a part of her complex message to others.

⌒

Meanwhile, during all these comings and goings, there was a major storm brewing at my home campus. After the departure of Ted Carpenter, an entirely new policy had been set down by the university authorities. No longer was the anthropology department encouraged, even required, to be an experimental arm of the university, testing out new curriculum ideas and new teaching methods; it was now to settle back into a safer approach and develop a conventional anthropology curriculum. Some faculty were dismissed or not rehired, others quit, and a new group of professors came in plainly set to reform the entire department.

I unhesitatingly went ahead doing what I thought I had been hired to do, but eventually the university president, a pleasant, even courtly gentleman, called me into his office and pointed out to me that I was the only member of the full-time faculty who did not have a Ph.D. (or even an M.A., for that matter). He also said rather wistfully that when he had been a young professor, it was expected that no active faculty member would stay longer on the same campus than perhaps four or five years before going somewhere else for a more advanced rank or different duties. Nowadays, he said, young faculty expect to spend their entire professional lives at a single institution— and I had to agree that I had not thought of moving along either. Actually, it turned out that I had been retained to date under the so-called Einstein Law, passed by the California legislature when it was pointed out to them that Einstein himself did not have the qualifications to teach elementary physics in an American state university. The only other person in the entire state besides me who was teaching in such a disgraceful un-degreed condition turned out to be Charles Seeger—Pete's father and an eminent musicologist. I felt very special to be thought of in such company.

A minor storm erupted when the word got out that I might be fired. Many, many letters were received from past and present students—phone calls, the whole works. I never saw any of this or knew who, if anyone, was organizing the protest; just the knowledge of it was comforting, and it enabled me to sit back and review my situation more carefully. Finally, I went to the president and made him a proposal: that I would go to another college and achieve at least an M.A., if he would promise me at least another year's teaching at SFV when I returned. We shook hands on it, and I set forth to try to matriculate in anthropology at the University of California at Berkeley.

To my surprise, my application was denied. Of course, the Berkeley anthropology department was at that time quite prestigious, with a very attractive faculty, and the graduate program was highly competitive. But to be turned down was an awfully educational experience in itself. The grounds for my rejection were interesting: essentially, they thought I was too old. A more appealing consideration that they also offered was that I already had an ongoing career: I had published and read papers at scholarly meetings, therefore I didn't really need graduate work.

But I did need it. So I telephoned an old friend, Dr. Alan Dundes, chairman of the Berkeley folklore program, and asked if I could do graduate work in his part of the department. He was encouraging and hospitable, as always, so Butch and I packed up in the summer of 1969, rented our Santa Monica house out for a year, and made off for the Berkeley campus, where we already felt a bit at home. And it turned out to be a great year, especially for me.

I found that I adored graduate school, that I was now old enough and experienced enough in the ways of academia to grab hold of the tempting possibilities that confronted me and work out a program that filled in at least some of my deficiencies. Being around Alan Dundes for a year was an education in itself. Having nothing to do but go to classes and write papers was totally pleasurable. The best part of all, I think, was that I had determined early on not to let my lovely time be wasted. If a class didn't seem to be what I needed, I could tell within one or two sessions and go and get into another equally promising course without delay. I felt totally in charge—unlike my fellow graduate students, who spent far too much of their irreplaceable time sitting in the graduate student reading room feeling powerless and bewailing their variously sad fates. Most pleasant of all was participating in several seminars with my daughter Naomi, also a graduate student (one year ahead of me!) in the anthropology department. She was working on primate behavior, and we argued across the seminar table just as we did back home, and I was accused of pointing my finger at her a time or two.

As time went on, I realized that to achieve my M.A. degree, I would have to write a proper thesis. Now was the moment, I decided, to work on that "Happy Birthday to You" business. With the entire UC Berkeley library at my disposal, I gleefully started in, only to discover I had barely scratched the surface in my preliminary studies. As so often has happened to me, there was so much more to the topic than I had realized, and there were also sources that even the Berkeley library didn't have available. I began to flounder.

But I worked and worked and worked, and my advisory committee kept helping, and I finally emerged with a lengthy (although still anthropologically incomplete) thesis. As I look back on it, I also can see that it was written in a somewhat sophomoric style, mostly because so much of the information was so fresh to me that I hadn't quite digested it and so resorted to the slightly girlish style that tended often to lie beneath my writing. But my kindly faculty committee accepted it, and it was duly shelved in the Berkeley library along with all the other M.A. theses for all time. I got my M.A. in one year and I went triumphantly home to San Fernando Valley State College and almost everybody was pretty happy, some more than others.

I decided to deliver a paper on the results of my investigations at one of the upcoming annual meetings of the American Folklore Society. It was very well received and listeners urged me to have it published in a journal, but somehow I never could decide what to do with it next. The original thesis still needed work, I believed, and was still too long to be practical; without its academic setting, a short version would be unacceptable by a professional journal without full footnotes and bibliography. Because of its unconventional approach, though, I couldn't think of an unacademic publication that might accept it. Besides all that, I found that I felt I had said all I had to say on that matter anyway and really wanted to get on to another topic.

But people kept on asking when they could get hold of a copy and I kept on thinking of it as an unfinished issue myself. In fact I still do. I'll end this chapter with a greatly abridged version of my thesis.

⌒⌒

Some years ago—the date isn't important—I happened to see a group of Mexican American young men being interviewed by a local television reporter on the steps of a courthouse. They had been charged with some criminal activity, and all were wearing handcuffs and leg irons. Each was asked his name and age. One said, "My name is . . . and I am nineteen years old today." "Oh," the reporter said. "Well, happy birthday!" The prisoner said, "Thank you," and the interview went on. No one seemed to find the exchange at all ironic.

The social necessity of wishing someone a happy birthday and the consequent inference that a birthday is pretty important business had become apparent to me some time before when I had found that the song "Happy Birthday to You" was the only song that everybody seemed able to agree could properly be called a folksong. It met all the classical criteria: everyone not only knew it, they felt somehow that they always had; no one could ever remember having been "taught" it; and everyone had heard a variation on it from time to time. I became intrigued by its universality.

Considered dispassionately, it isn't a very interesting song. It's brief, repetitive in text, and commonplace in many ways actually uncharacteristic of the general American style of song writing and song singing. It's excessively redundant, and American songs tend toward the wordy; it's most frequently sung by groups and American songs tend toward the solo, both in construction and in performance. Still it's one of the few songs we ever sing in public. At ball games and conventions even the National Anthem is rarely sung with any fervor, but I have heard an entire restaurant full of diners break spontaneously and loudly into "Happy Birthday to You" when a lighted cake was being carried to a table.

At one point I even wondered if perhaps there simply weren't any better birthday songs available, but a look at a few song-finding lists soon disabused me of that notion. Hundreds of other birthday songs have been written—we simply never sing them (although there are some interesting recent variations cropping up in the Spanish-speaking community).

The hypothesis occurred to me that perhaps the banal text and the bland melody of "Happy Birthday to You" might have some especially elegant fit with the basic American concept of the nature of the birthday event. Perhaps the verbal folklore item—the song that embodies in its text the standard formulaic birthday greeting—might prove to be a kind of publicly stated, group-sponsored paradigm of the really critical elements in the overall social custom.

Methodologically, this struck me as a neat and elegant little problem. In practice, it led me into a kind of "Golden Bough" exploration, with no end to the possibilities of adventure.

I started out by investigating the history of the song itself. Having never been attracted to the nineteenth-century concept that folksongs are simply lower-class versions of upper-class artistic products (sometimes called *gesunkenes Kulturgut*), it is annoying to have to admit that "Happy Birthday to You" is an excellent example of this notion. A second blow to my morale came with the clear evidence that the song was not archaic, not anonymous, and not even particularly old, all of which I had somewhat patronizingly assumed.

It had first appeared in 1898 in the form of a parent song, "Good Morning to All" (a song still known in kindergarten circles) in a volume titled *Song Stories for the Kindergarten and Nursery School* prepared by two maiden schoolteachers, one of whom was so distinguished that her death in 1936 was noted by a full column obituary in the *New York Times*.

Miss Mildred J. Hill, the composer of the team, is listed in the ASCAP biographical dictionary as a "church organist, concert pianist, and authority on Negro spirituals." Further, she worked with her younger sister, Miss Patty, as a music teacher in the latter's experimental kindergarten training school. Patty Smith Hill, the lyricist, was perhaps a more vigorous woman, clearly possessed of daring, determination, and intellectual ability. Her formal education ended with her graduation from high school in 1887, at which time she began her life as a kindergarten teacher. A dedicated and unregenerate Dewey-ite, her radical and successful innovations in both curriculum and methodology were so impressive that she was eventually invited to join the faculty of Teachers College at Columbia University, which also awarded her the honorary degree of Doctor of Letters.

Miss Patty was a president of the Association for Childhood Education and the first chair of the National Association for Nursery Education. Her literary output includes *Experimental Studies in Kindergarten Theory and Practice* and, with Vera Fedievsky, *Nursery School and Parent Education in Soviet Russia*, published in 1936. But despite her undoubted professional achievements, her most influential literary productions will probably prove to be the two brief songs for which she provided the lyrics, "Good Morning to All" and "Happy Birthday to You."

It has proven curiously difficult, in fact impossible, to determine at just what point after the 1893 publication of *Song Stories for the Kindergarten and Primary Schools* Miss Patty set the lyric lines now known as "Happy Birthday to You" to the melody of "Good Morning to All." Since it all happened so relatively recently, it's frustrating to find that apparently nobody ever asked her, or if they did she didn't say. Given her profession and overall educational philosophy, it seems likely that the parody lines simply evolved in some kindergarten classroom under her general aegis. In any event, the first publication record is not until 1935, when "The Happy Birthday March" by Mildred H. and Patty S. Hill was printed in sheet music form, without lyrics, by the Summy Publishing Company, then of Chicago, which followed it in 1939 with the publication of a sheet music edition with lyrics.

There followed immediately a whole rash of litigations instigated by the Summy Company over the problem of copyright infringement, the most prominent being against Irving Berlin, who had, in all apparent innocence, used "Happy Birthday to You" in a skit in his Broadway review *As Thousands Cheer.* The authors of *Panama Hattie* and *The Male Animal* also paid up handsomely, and it is to be hoped that Patty Hill's retirement years were comfortable indeed.

The point is that, even as early as 1935, most people simply assumed (as I certainly would have) that "Happy Birthday to You" was a folksong, or at least old enough to be in the public domain. Even the telegraph companies thought so. The singing telegram service was inaugurated in 1936, and "Happy Birthday to You" became widely known throughout Western Union as "the cake taker." By 1941, it was estimated that it had been sung at least a million and a half times by the telegraph minstrels alone.

One of the striking features of the story just outlined concerns the overall speed of events. In the area of folklore one grows accustomed to thinking in terms of the majestic procession of centuries. "Happy Birthday to You" became firmly established as a "folksong" in the popular mind within a period of forty years at the absolute outside limit. And if one considers that the "Happy Birthday" lyric was written sometime after 1893, and that the song was fully accepted as a folksong sometime before 1933, ten or even twenty years could be shaved off at a conservative estimate.

I suspect that the historical biases of most folklorists lead us to think of the tradition-establishing process as far more lengthy and cumbersome than it actually is. One of the many things I learned when my children were small was that only by the most agile footwork on my part was I able to avoid establishing traditions on an almost hourly basis. Human beings—the "pattern makers and the pattern perceivers," as they were once characterized—start work at their basic job from the moment of birth.

The critical element, then, is not the initiation of a tradition, but its dissemination and its acceptance. The question of dissemination or spread, it seems to me, has already been taken care of. It is difficult even to hypothesize two more speedy and effective agents of mass circulation than what Iona and Peter Opie call the "schoolchild underground" and the entire wireless telegraph industry. But a song not only has to move, it also, in a sense, has to stay still: it must be remembered. It has to fit.

In tackling the problem of mass acceptance, it seems appropriate first to scrutinize closely the item being disseminated. I started with the music, and will report only briefly that when Miss Mildred composed her brief tune, she hit precisely in the center of a large cluster of American musical norms. For example, out of twelve of the pertinent characteristics listed by Jan Philip Schinhan in *The Music of the Songs and Ballads in the Frank C. Brown Collection*, Miss Mildred's tune conforms to nine exactly and is well within range on the remaining three. In other words, she was successful in writing a melody that most Americans can feel comfortable singing, since it falls well within the dimensions of our overall opinions as to what a melody "ought" to be.

The same thing cannot be said exactly of the lyrics, which are not only rudimentary, but which make the same statement four times running with only one slight variation. Some degree of repetition, of course, characterizes all oral literature, but some genres and some societies seem to hold it as more important than others. Overall, redundancy does not seem to be a stressed characterizer of American song style—the very existence of the narrative ballad as an important song form indicates otherwise. The extent of redundancy in the lyric of "Happy Birthday to You" may indicate, then, either that the Misses Hill were playing about with the non-normal (as all creative people must do to some extent) or that the redundant statement is simply so important that it can stand being repeated four times.

If one stops laughing and really takes a hard look at the verbal content of the statement "Happy birthday to you," one is struck by what a limited remark it is. It contains no whisper of past deeds nor of future prospects, no congratulations, no good wishes beyond the day. Yesterday you could have done something hateful or magnificent, cowardly or great-hearted. Tomorrow I may wish you either well or ill. But today—and today only—you get a happy birthday.

This highly restricted statement is also directed toward only one individual by virtue of the song's inclusion, as the only departure from almost total redundancy, of the name of the particular birthday celebrant. Indeed, on occasions when the song is sung by a group, each person singing tends to use the name by which he normally addresses the individual in direct conversation. The resultant cacophony ("Happy birthday dear Daddy / Mister Jones / John / Grandpa / Uncle John") makes even more explicit the essential function of the lyric line: to convey a rigorously limited statement from a single individual to another single individual.

Paradoxically, the restricted melodic range, the four-square metric construction, and the single and not overly difficult vocal leap make the melody admirably suitable for group singing; it is actually awkward to sing it alone. It may be possible that one of the reasons for the song's remarkable attractiveness to Americans is that it presents an exact paradigm of one of the principal ways in which we often think of groups: as temporary assemblages of discrete units, coincidental collections of separate and distinct individuals.

In passing, it's instructive to see what happens to our song when it is translated into other languages, for "Happy Birthday to You" is close to being an international favorite. I myself have only scanty evidence as to how widely it is sung or how popular it is—and I suspect that some of its translations are the work of missionaries and the like—still, "Happy Birthday to You" does exist in tongues as improbable as Tagalog and Yoruba.

In more than one Spanish-speaking country one sings "Feliz

cumpleaños para tí," and it is significant that the term "cumpleaños" (in contrast to "aniversario" or "natividad") is translatable
as "completion of many years"—a clear suggestion of past and
future. In Holland one sings forthrightly "Long may he live,
long may he live, long may he live in prosperity, hip hip hooray!"
In Ewe the song goes "May birthday's blessings be yours, may
many more years be yours, one year after another, may God
bless you."

Throughout the twenty-five or so translations I have casually
accumulated, one invariably observes more linguistic content
than in the original. They are more complex, less redundant,
and all contain references to past or future or both. None speak
of the birthday in the same isolated way that the American version does, as though the birthday were a frozen chunk of time,
a spatially separate twenty-four-hour unit.

The restricted nature of the American message on the other
hand—"I (independently) wish you (individually) a rigorously
limited time period (twenty-four hours, no more, no less) of
happiness without reference to what you have accomplished in
the past nor to what you may do in the future"—explains how
Americans can, with perfect aplomb and a complete absence of
irony, wish a prisoner in chains a "happy birthday." It is also why
we can sit in a restaurant and sing "Happy Birthday to You" to
some total stranger we can't even see across the room. There's
nothing personal about it at all. To Americans, every dog has
his day and every human being gets a birthday once a year. All
you have to do is to be alive at the right time.

Is that what we're celebrating? Is that, as has been said in
another connection, all there is? Well, that's what the song
says—that stupid little "folksong" that everybody knows—and
I think it's right on the money. Many people have spoken of the
"birthday" under the general anthropological category of a rite
of passage, and perhaps it may be, in some societies or on some
special occasions. But in general, I believe this categorization to
be in error here. Certainly, the overall form of the celebration
suggests a passing rite; however, several distinctive features of the
American birthday concept suggest otherwise. The birthday celebrant is not expected to be himself altered by the experience for

one thing, nor is his social condition any different than before. Besides, the condition of having a birthday is neither achieved by the individual nor conferred by the culture. It simply occurs annually throughout the life span.

Thus the American birthday appears to function as a ceremony of individual social recognition. Once a year, Americans seem to feel a social compulsion to say to each person separately: you are alive; I greet you; I hope you're happy about it all.

The limitations, the "lack" of content of the birthday message, become therefore very important. If life itself—the simple condition of being alive rather than dead—is what is being celebrated, then you can't qualify it. Great deeds and noble accomplishments have nothing to do with it.

It is the very impersonality of the American birthday wish that makes its fundamental humanism possible. You have to neither know nor like the individual to be able to honor the fact that he exists, if that's all you're doing; nor do you have to feel you must wish him well in future. The day after his birthday, he can fall and break a leg, or you can do him down in a business deal or completely ignore his existence. But on his birthday he is there, simply there, and attention must be paid.

I have to admit that I started out this project not liking birthdays very much. They seemed to me trivial, full of greed and commercialism, featuring a kind of "Queen for a Day" shallowness and glitz. But as I've grown older, I've gained much more respect for the overall delicacy of the cultural fabric that holds us all together. It's a fabric made up of subtly interwoven and complex cultural compromises, and it has begun to seem to me that where the birthday fits in is as a mediating influence between two very contradictory aspects of American society: our fundamental and very deep-seated egalitarianism (still, I believe, a strong force in American thought), and our insistence on unrestrained competitive individualism.

The two don't fit together very comfortably, as the history of the United States over the past two hundred years has shown. But the birthday ceremonial and its associated song say: every year, every citizen (good, bad, or indifferent) must be honored by his society for the simple fact of his existence as a social unit.

There is, it seems to me, a kind of reluctant nobility of concept here. I hope it survives.

And so, this seems to me to be why all Americans know and sing "Happy Birthday to You." It is brief and undemanding—as a "ceremonial" song, it's a joke—but it's one of our few songs constructed for a group to sing to an individual, which is what we want to do on a birthday. It is not sentimental or poetically conceived; we would be publicly embarrassed if it were, and a lot of people wouldn't sing it. It's as tight-lipped and as flatly democratic as the millions of Americans who do sing it each year. And above all, it says, exactly and precisely (no more, no less) just what we want to say. For if it said any more, it could not say as much: Happy birthday to you.

Guitar class at the Westside Jewish Community Center, Los Angeles: tape recorder day. (Photo by Marvin A. Lyons)

Teaching at San Fernando Valley State College.

Naomi, Bess, and Corey at UCLA, early 1960s. (Photo by Wayland Hand)

Bess with Margaret Mead at the Smithsonian Folklife Festival, Washington, D.C., 1976.

Bessie Jones and children at the Smithsonian Folklife Festival, Washington, D.C., 1976.

Bess and Alan Lomax at the inauguration of President Jimmy Carter,
Washington, D.C., 1977. (Photo © 2006 Roland L. Freeman)

Bess escorted by son Nick to the state dinner for National Medal of Arts
recipients, Washington, D.C., 1993.

President Bill Clinton, Bess, and Hillary Rodham Clinton at the National Medal of Arts ceremony, White House Rose Garden, 1993.

TEN

The Smithsonian Festivals

Suddenly, everything changed. My husband, artist and songwriter Butch Hawes, died unexpectedly in December 1971. He was only fifty-two and I was only fifty. He had spent most of his life combating a crippling arthritis, but he had never stopped drawing and writing. He had fathered three interesting and productive children; he had helped build a busy and happy family. He had produced some fine new songs, a series of black-and-white drawings and cartoons for the freelance market, some compelling charcoal portraits, and, in the last years, a group of exciting wax sculptures that I later had cast in bronze. He left me comfortably situated in my university teaching; our three grown children were variously engaged in undergraduate work, graduate research, parenting, and first jobs. All his life he had kept on showing up to do what he thought he ought to do, but finally he had run his race and he left his house in order. He keeps turning up every once in a while in my dreams.

For the first two years after my husband's death, I mostly tried to keep my suddenly flaccid life from further collapse. Teaching is what I did and do, and so teaching was what I kept on doing. But then Ralph Rinzler, an old friend from my folksong singing days, called me from Washington, D.C., and asked me to prepare a living presentation of the arts traditional to the "California heartland" (which he roughly defined as the agricultural and fishing areas from just north of San Francisco to just south of San Diego) and present it in the "Regional America" section of the Smithsonian Institution's annual Festival of American Folklife, held in the capital. I kept saying that I didn't know anything about that area and had never organized even one concert, but Ralph could be mighty persuasive. And then all my life I had tried out things I had never done before (*Faciendo ediscere facere*).

So I agreed to give it a try and suggested to my senior folklore seminar that we might take on the planning of it as a semester group project. The students were interested, and away we went. I asked them first to collect all the statistical information about the area they could amass, including the historical dimensions, and the data just began to pour in. We never got it all sorted out properly, but the plunge into the records was totally refreshing to all of us, especially me, I believe. We concentrated first on trying to figure out at least a few of the vital and compelling characteristics of the area, and the ones we hit upon at least gave me some starting points for later program planning. (We never completed all we were trying to do, of course. In later years I was to contemplate how only the academic world ever allows an investigator even a fraction of the time actually needed to do what you are supposed to be doing.)

The first and, to me, most critically important characteristic we hit upon was the year-round growing cycle. Southern California is one of the "garden spots" of the world, because there is *always* an array of highly desirable eatables and usables coming into bloom, ripening, drying up, seeding, and doing it all over again. Olives and oranges, rice and cotton, lettuce and garlic and grapes and avocados and tomatoes—there is hardly anything growable that won't thrive in this fortunate part of the world. Naturally this has deeply affected who came there, when they came, and just where they settled down. At one time or another, everybody seems to have wanted to come to California and do their favorite thing. Dairy people wanted to produce milk and cheese, vintners wanted to grow grapes, fishing people wanted to harvest the profusion of coastal fish and mollusks.

And then, when the newcomers' little vineyard or vegetable plantation was properly located and running and they needed more help, what better could they do than to write back home and see if a couple of unemployed nephews and nieces couldn't come over and help out? The unstoppable desire of people to get their own folks together seems to have been one of the major factors in the very early appearance of California "minority" communities in the rural areas and "ethnic" neighborhoods in the cities.

So although it is now a commonplace for large areas to enclose many different groups of people with varying cultures speaking varying languages, central and southern California was originally settled in a hodgepodge sort of way. Americans from other parts of the United States (including African Americans) got to California very early, but there they also met early groups of Russians, Portuguese, Filipinos, Armenians, Italians, Mexicans from several parts of Mexico, Chinese, Japanese, and Irish, among others. A number of now-decimated American Indian tribes also once roamed the arid land around what is now San Diego.

The year-round growth cycle soon required large numbers of farm laborers, but by the time this was generally apparent most of the farm/residential properties had been bought up, resulting in the appearance of enormous numbers of temporary workers who moved through the state following the crop harvests. That meant that a large part of the state population was truly mobile, with little chance of settling down anywhere. That really hadn't happened often before. We hear so much now about the problems of migrant labor that we don't realize how unique California's situation has been. Compare, for instance, the New England states, where perhaps they will need to bring in harvesters for the apple crop or the like; but that ends the possibilities for much work, and all those extra people have to move on and look for work somewhere else.

And besides, there were the city folks to think about, and the special California occupations that had their own folklore too. I began to feel that there was no way to present all this complexity respectably well, but Ralph kept urging me on. He kept telling me that I was just conducting a talent hunt, that I shouldn't get things too complicated, and of course he was right.

But it was obvious I was going to have to prepare some kind of a multicultural presentation, and thus I clearly needed some expert assistance. I began to look not only for performers, but for cultural workers. I was especially concerned about the presentations involving Mexican Americans, since their numbers and influence were so great; I myself was unqualified to uncover that talent, most particularly since I had no Spanish. I sent out all kinds of inquiries for a seasoned expert in Chicano (the term used at the time) music and/or dance, and one day I was called up by a UCLA ethnomusicology graduate student.

We had quite a conversation. I started out by describing what I was supposed to be pulling together, said that I was especially anxious that as wide a range of Mexican American musical styles as possible should be included, and inquired about what he already knew was available in Southern California. He began telling me about an itinerant corrido singer/composer he had run into in Los Angeles, who had a great traditional repertory, but who had recently moved and nobody knew quite where he was. However the old gentleman's girlfriend worked in a taco stand on the corner of Figueroa and something street on the 2:00 A.M. shift; if I was interested, my new telephonic friend said, he would be glad to stop by some night and see if she had any information as to where the corrido singer had gone.

I immediately thought to myself, "What I have on the phone here is a genuine field-worker," and I arranged an early meeting. His name was Daniel Sheehy. He was Irish and had been born in Bakersfield, where he had run with the neighborhood Mexican American kids throughout his growing up. He became fluent in their language, their ways, and their music, and had been overwhelmed to find that there was a university where he could actually get credit for doing what he was already doing and already loved. He made it into the music department at UCLA, and when I met him he had completed preliminary work on his doctoral dissertation in the Department of Ethnomusicology. He was one of my great finds—a knowledgeable, conscientious, gentle man, with a scholar's experience and a humanist's impetuous heart. He also projected an infectious kind of joy in music, whether he was listening to it, recording it, or playing it himself. From the time I first met him until today he has been playing in one or another mariachi ensemble, and I know him so well I can recognize when his current group of *compadres* has not been active for a while: he is clearly not himself, and he needs to go play some music somewhere with somebody.

Dan took over the Hispanic problem with imagination and energy, locating an irresistible mariachi, an impressively loud *banda* (a small group of parade-leading brass players), some gorgeously suited *charros* (Mexican "rodeo" riders), a group of teenagers learning mural painting at a community cultural center as an alternative to other forms of wall decoration, several farmworker *corridistas* (ballad singers), paper flower and piñata makers, and cooks. Other field-workers brought in old-timey fiddlers and string players, a fine traditional black gospel quartet, a blues piano player, an improbable but prosperous group of Assyrians from San Francisco whose women used spindles to spin their knitting skeins out of nylon fleece rather than hard-to-find wool (a situation they thought I should do something about), and men who played the frame drums and clarinet-type instruments used throughout the Near East. Then there were two groups of traditional Portuguese: one from the dairy community of central California (for whom the Smithsonian brought in some cows so that they could be decorated with paper flowers and garlands for a traditional parade at the end of the week), and one from a fishing community near San Diego (whose local traditional boat builder carved a model boat and duly sailed it across the Reflecting Pool in front of the Washington Monument). On top of all this glory, there were the Chinese kite maker, the Filipino yo-yo player (one of the original group that popularized the game back in the 1920s and 30s), the urban scissors sharpener with his little pushcart (working away on a stock of dull cutlery the local Smithsonian staff were glad to have repaired), two Greek straw-beehive makers, and a cable car bellringer from San Francisco (who appeared complete with cable car to show the jazzy style of bell ringing that had developed for the annual bell-ringing contest).

There were some things we found we just couldn't do. We couldn't bring the charros' horses, so their contribution had to be reduced to trick-roping demonstrations (but they still were great crowd pleasers and highly decorative). We couldn't present any of the California Indian communities we visited: their traditions had been sadly neglected, and the only demonstrator they seemed to want to send was simply too old and frail to withstand the journey. But we did get a small "wall" built and a mural painted upon it by the group of Chicano teenagers; and—most special, in a way, of all—we did persuade representatives from a Russian Molokan community, a singular and secluded group that had been harried from their homes through China before improbably reaching Brazil and finally the United States and Canada, carrying all that way a matchless tradition of hymns sung in a matchless improvised four-part harmony. This was the first time they had ever appeared in public, except for one concert in their own town. They told me at the end of the festival that they had decided God had told them to come. I deeply hope they have never been sorry; we tried very hard not to violate their traditional privacy.

During the fast-moving weeks we were actually on the National Mall, everyone performed splendidly. The muralists painted, Scissors Sam sharpened, the blues player in his little private glade played so lovingly that many people stayed with him all day long, the Portuguese decorated their gorgeous black-and-white cows with equally gorgeous multicolored crepe paper garlands and bunches of flowers, and the whole contingent—followed by all who cared to join in—marched down the length of the Reflecting Pool (with music provided by the banda) to the African Diaspora church and back again for a midmorning feast of fresh-baked cookies and milk.

As so frequently happens, though, the unforgettable moments took place during a real crisis. Washington is known for sudden and violent electrical storms accompanied by gully-washing downpours of rain, and the entire Smithsonian staff knew that immediate emergency steps had to be taken to protect the participants and the equipment, most especially anything that was plugged in or could blow over. Such a storm hit us one afternoon, almost before the weather forecasters could warn us, and it was inspiring to see everyone in the Regional America section—musicians, dancers, sound technicians, *everybody*—running immediately for the mural (nearly finished on its enormous canvas "wall") and lugging it away to safety. Before the phones were cut off, somebody had called for the buses; they rolled up, massive and dry, and our drenched and frightened participants, clutching their instruments and paintbrushes, were transported safely "home" to the somewhat bleak and modernistic university dormitory housing we had leased. Morale was pretty low, I'm afraid. The electricity was off and no one knew when, if ever, we could see again. But then we heard that great choral sound that could come only from the Molokans echoing through the huge building. It turned out that as the sun went down and everything was turning black and the wind began to die, they had gathered in the stairwell next to their suite of rooms and sung to themselves and to us all, their exquisitely blended voices echoing up and down the empty stairs, assuring each one of us that we were not alone. It was a moment no one will ever forget. And sure enough, the lights did come back on and everybody went in to supper.

⌒

The entire California show had been a wonderful, though exhausting, experience and I began to feel that I had learned how to do such things a little bit. And then Ralph came up to me and asked if I would now consider taking over a newly made position: assistant director for presentation at the 1976 Festival of American Folklife. I already knew this was to be an event of unparalleled complexity and interest, the kind of thing it was almost impossible to turn down. My old anthropology friends at CSUN urged me to apply for a sabbatical year for the purpose. I did, and I got it.

For a long time, the year 1976 had been heralded as an occasion for national celebration, and almost every institution and community across the country had planned special projects in honor of "American's big birthday."

But somehow the spirit got lost in the planning, or in the election campaign, or in the national traumas of the 1950s and 60s. Very few people seemed enthusiastic about any kind of party. All kinds of quarrels developed as to where the money for all these nice ideas was to come from, and there was lots of quibbling about how our forefathers weren't all that spotless and celebration-worthy anyway, and really, was stopping off for this two-hundredth birthday the very best way of spending federal and state monies? It seemed as though no matter how big and gorgeous the occasion, nobody truly wanted to come.

However the Smithsonian seems to be the one federal institution that can serenely rise above almost anything, in large part because (as I had discovered during the previous summer's California fieldwork) it appears to have permanently acquired the trust and confidence of the American people. As soon as a field-worker said, "The Smithsonian invites you . . . ," the most improbable kinds of people accepted with pleasure. They all seemed to know what the Smithsonian was and they were ready to go.

So the Bicentennial Festival was planned as a humdinger, a barn burner, a truly national celebration, as big and as beautiful as the country itself. It was to run the entire summer—twelve weeks in all. We started out, I believe, with a budget of $3,000,000 (a colossal amount of money at that time) and ended up with more than $7,000,000 expended. Appropriately, a national airline and a national food-producing company kicked in $1,000,000 apiece, and the Congress and the Smithsonian itself contributed heavily also.

The closest thing I can think of to the 1976 festival would have to be a combination of the summer and winter Olympic Games of any recent year. Both the Folklife Festival and the Olympics produce exemplary demonstrations of the possibility that a vast variety of nations and cultures can assemble without making war. Both events make serious attempts to include appropriate representation for everybody (although some will always decline to participate for fiscal, political, or cultural reasons). Every participating group is invited to show off its skills in activities that its members are proud of and feel good about making public. Both celebrations have deep-laid, historically based organizing principles—neither is a hodgepodge. And everyone who participates wants to do it again and goes home talking about next year.

I can say the foregoing about the 1976 festival with some assurance because I somehow became the Smithsonian representative who met at the end of each week with the departing participants to thank them for coming, admired once again their exceptional arts and performances, and wished them a safe journey home . . . and then turned to give a formal greeting to the oncoming wave of craftspeople, singers, dancers, and cultural specialists for the next seven days (an estimated five thousand individuals came through during those twelve weeks of summer). But the Smithsonian had already produced a folklife festival on the Mall for nine years and had learned something about how to make the vast jumble of cultures and skills into reasonably coherent pictures.

The underlying structures on the Mall were both strong *and* flexible (a principle I would discover to be of enormous importance in my later work at the National Endowment for the Arts). There were five major presentation sites: Native America, African Diaspora, Working America, Old Ways in the New World (primarily European and Asian), and Regional America—each with its own responsibility, rationale, and character. In addition, there were several smaller presentation areas: the Children's Area, Family Folklore (where visitors could record their own family traditions), and a Main Stage for special performances attracting larger crowds. Within each area, appropriate food was sold to consumers and its preparation freely demonstrated to those interested. Some food, like some individual performances, circulated through the entire festival—for example, the fresh fruit sold by the Baltimore arabbers from their traditional pony-drawn carts.

From the artists' and the audience's perspectives, each of the five major areas presented different strategies for looking at cultural activities and how they reflected their communities. Old Ways tried to assemble both immigrant and stay-at-home artists so they could compare performances and experiences. Each week, Working America presented different industries (transportation, building, communications, for example), discussed and demonstrated by the appropriate unions and independent workers. Native America wanted representatives from every different tribe to be present to show their varying lifestyles and their remarkably preserved and developed artistic traditions. Each week African Diaspora brought representatives from an African region, a black South American people, and the black United States in order to investigate their interrelated histories and cultural development. And Regional America wanted to take a cross-cultural slice of each of the large geographic/cultural areas we all recognize when talking about the nation (for example, the Deep South, the Far West, and Appalachia). Overall, it made for an awfully interesting take on the present, past, and future.

Each participant presented many different programming possibilities.

Most could have settled in happily in two or three different areas. After all, everybody had to have some kind of a job sometime (Working America), everybody had to live in some particular part of the United States (Regional America), and everybody had come here from some other place in the world (African Diaspora and Old Ways in the New World). The Native Americans, who had been here first, fit in anywhere and could go anywhere. The Smithsonian staff had to help develop the most appropriate background in which the enormously varied artists whom they invited to visit the capital could demonstrate their special ideas.

I personally most welcomed the occasions when artists themselves would make creative contacts across festival location boundaries. They had to work pretty fast to get acquainted in no more than seven days, but this gave them a chance to demonstrate a bit of their complex identities. One week, the staff had brought in both black and white working cowboys from Texas; they and their horses and some local heifers happily occupied the Regional America barn. The Mexican American charros, who were also part of the Regional America presentation that week, tended to be a bit reserved, but there is something about real horses than draws horsemen together, and eventually some pretty interesting conversations developed over horse quality, knot tying, roping styles, and the like. It turned out that the Mescalero Apaches, themselves famous horsemen, were being presented in Native America, and some of those fellows too began dropping by to visit and talk over the Smithsonian's ideas of what makes an exhibitable horse and various methods of handling yearlings. Everybody was getting along so well by the end of the week that when a beleaguered heifer broke free of the corral and raced for freedom, a joyfully whooping cross-cultural posse (including some happy Park Service mounted police) spontaneously took after her and finally managed to rope her on the grounds of the Kennedy Center.

Of course, that's an easy one when you look back on it. But the amount of planning and effort it took to have those varied fellows and their horses and the young cattle in place on the Mall at the same time, everybody feeling like they were comfortable enough to have some fun right there in the shadow of the Washington Monument . . . well, it all took some doing, not to mention the fact that the various staffs had done enough careful observation and knew their folks well enough to just let the celebration go on its own happy way.

Then there were the two coopers (barrel makers), from Tennessee and Japan, respectively, who met on the Mall and developed such admiration of each other's craftsmanship that they visited almost daily either in Old Ways or Regional America. After the festival was over they corresponded, and they eventually arranged trips to see each other's country and to meet still other members of their profession. We never had enough staff or money or time to follow what happened when *all* those five thousand people got home. But the few we know about, at least, got home safely and had lots of stories to tell their grandchildren.

⌐⌐

The entire 1976 festival was simply too big and too complicated and too adventurous to be easily described in full or detail. I do not believe anyone who ever worked on the Mall that long summer was ever the same afterward. It profoundly affected me, I know. As assistant director for presentation, my work had really been done, I felt, by the time the big event started—each of the areas was professionally and competently staffed, and now the crystallization of the ideas was really up to them.

I had, I hope, learned a good bit in the year between the summers of 1975 and 1976. At Ralph's urging, I had switched from my California perspective to a necessarily larger one, and I naively assumed my new presence would be welcomed by the experienced staff that were already on board, some of them for a year or two. As I look back now, I cannot conceive how I could have been so blind as to believe that all these hardworking people would accept with pleasure the arrival of a new and untested right hand for their beloved and inspirational boss, Ralph Rinzler. I had spent the year between the two summers trying to stay out of the way while pushing things forward (there was always a mountain of work to be done), making everyone feel as good as possible under these awkward circumstances, and putting in any ideas I might have in such a way that they could both be taken seriously and easily left behind. In other words, I was trying to get accepted into the staff as a coworker, and gradually things got better and I began to feel I was perhaps a bit of a help—every once in a while.

When the festival actually began in June 1976 I again found myself without a job description—not that I ever had had a full one—so I just started stepping into places where I saw gaps. After each welcoming or good-bye day, I tried to circulate through the whole festival, introducing myself and shaking hands with every participant I could scare up in each area. Apparently they recognized me, enjoyed my brief visits, and began to save up things they wanted to ask about or get done. For instance, almost everyone in Native America the whole summer long wanted to find a grandparent's medicine bundle or bead collar they had always heard had been given to the Smithsonian. I got in touch with the Native America staff, and they with the museum curators, and thanks to the incredible diligence of the museologists I don't believe there was a single failure in locating these long ago bequests. A museum staffer would come over and guide the folks personally to the proper building, and the next day when I wandered by again, someone would come to me with shining eyes and say, "I saw it. After all those years, I saw it. It was in a little drawer with his name on a card. And they let me take a picture!" It gave me renewed respect for the Smithsonian's accession and storage systems and the realization that the American people have just cause to be proud that their national museum not only accepts things, but keeps them and protects them.

I tried to take in a musical event or two from each musician on the Mall every week just to be in the audience and to congratulate performers and staff for their great contributions. I also began my still-active monitoring of sound. Sound interference from stage to stage was an enormous problem throughout the summer, with many delicate solos being drowned out by an enthusiastic drum choir around the corner. Each stage, even the small ones, had its own sound system and sound technician, but many of the latter had only worked with rock bands and were used to cranking the gain up nice and loud and then going off for a soda or reading a book. I explained endlessly that with folk and traditional music, as with classical music, the active attention of a sound technician was required throughout every moment, and that technician had to keep actively listening until the last sound faded away. I'm afraid I gained a reputation as some kind of a sound fanatic throughout the festival.

My visits to so many stages allowed me opportunities to chat with the singers and musicians. I noticed one morning that a young Scottish singer was scheduled for a half-hour's concert all by herself on the big stage. It seemed possible to me that this might be a bit daunting—she was barely five feet tall, with a sweet soft voice like a meadow lark, and she sang unaccompanied—so I dropped by in case she needed a friendly face around before she went on stage. She got very confiding: "You know, when I first came here with my little pocketful of songs and I heard all those marvelous things on the Mall—the big Indian drums, and the different string bands, and the religious choirs, and the African stringed instruments, and all that—I was really scared. But then each time I went out on stage and began to sing,

I realized deep down" (and here her voice got almost whispery, so as not to hurt anybody else's feelings) "that my songs were *really* the prettiest of them all!" I assured her that at that moment she was undoubtedly absolutely right, and I went on my way thinking that she had voiced the way all festival participants felt "deep down" about their music or their craft or their culture in general. All those other people's are wonderful, yes, but when you really come right down to it, one's own is where a person can find real satisfaction, and it's just a little tiny bit more special than anybody else's.

I had found that out in my own personal experience years before. I was attending a concert at the University of California at Los Angeles, a sampling of the musicians scheduled to appear in their occasional multiethnic arts festivals. It was held in the largest hall on the campus, which was packed, and it was truly impressive: kilted Scots bagpipers marched down the central aisle, African drummers thundered from the stage, mariachi orchestras blazed and trumpeted, gospel choirs filled the enormous hall with sonorities. I was in my element, making knowledgeable remarks to my companions, thrilling to each extraordinary set of sounds. The whole thing dragged on for hours until, almost at the end, three slightly bedraggled gentlemen carrying a banjo, a guitar, and a string bass shambled out on the stage, fussed around rather unprofessionally for a minute or two, and then struck up "Red Wing" . . . and my heart absolutely melted. The most extraordinary sense of total well-being came over me. I was comforted, I was secure, I was home, that was *my* song. And I realized to my embarrassment that if I had seen a copy of the program ahead of time, "Red Wing"—that corny fake-Indian love lyric with the infectious tune, played by thousands of southern fiddle bands—would have come down toward the bottom of my list. I had moved so far away from my roots, I had forgotten where they lay. But my roots had not forgotten; there they were ready to remind me who I am and where I come from. You can run away and pretend to be somebody else or even join another group, but your roots will always be there—holding no hard feelings either.

I hope that my old friend Ralph Rinzler felt as good as I did when it was all over. The Bicentennial Festival was his particular baby and he had started working on it five or six years before, first bringing in several remarkable assemblages of scholars in folklore, ethnomusicology, history, Americana, anthropology, and the like to develop the intellectual framework for the work to come. In the years to follow, Ralph personally took on the extremely difficult job of visiting all the nations who seemed interested in participating, explaining the concepts behind the festival, how we could *not* welcome the arrival of commercial troupes, persuading potential participants to tolerate the Smithsonian's sending in field-workers to select the craftspeople and musicians who would be invited. He also was in constant touch with their Washington embassies, as well as himself doing some of the American fieldwork.

As it came closer and closer to opening day, the tempo picked up, and then it became plain that he had decided his primary function during the festival itself was to be a troubleshooter. It seemed to me he spent most of his time in his Smithsonian office, or else over at the university dormitory where the participants were lodged and where the most difficult problems surfaced. I rarely saw him at performances, except for the largest and most difficult to bring off.

I began to believe that it was just too much for him to watch his creations coming to fruit. They had meant so much. He had invested so much of his energy and thought in the bicentennial celebration for so many years—and he had both to burn. Almost every morning of the year I worked in Washington, I would drop by his office and find him sitting at his desk chair jittering his leg (he was always jittering something) like some helium balloon longing to fly, held down to earth only by the cord of the telephone always at the ready on his shoulder, longing to put it to use, eager to hear the excitements, the problems, the complexities of the day, ready to spread the word, bursting with energy and life. I never worked with anyone quite like him. He was one of a kind, and he was the progenitor of the 1976 Bicentennial Festival—an unrepeatable and totally remarkable event.

On my first trip to Washington to meet with Ralph, he took me on a walk across the National Mall to show me the layout for the festival. He said, "Bess, I want to tell you some of the things I've learned in the past years about how to run festivals. There aren't very many of them, but I know they work." And he gave me an extraordinary and, to me, totally unexpected series of observations.

"First, never bring in big-name artists. Oh, they're wonderful, but if they're there, most of the people in the audience will have come to hear their woman or their man; and they can't open their hearts quite all the way to anybody else, they're so eager to hear their own. I want people coming to my festivals wondering what exciting *new* thing might happen, what terrific music that *next* band might play. I want an open-hearted audience.

"Then, anywhere you stand on the festival grounds I want people to be able to see or hear at least three different really interesting and attractive things going on—over here a gong orchestra (and whoever heard anything like that?), over there a string band (and you just love old-timey music), and over there some people dancing (and maybe you could get in and do it too). When there are a lot of truly enticing things going on, people will just drift toward the least crowded one, where they can get in closer, and so you don't need so much crowd control. The crowd controls itself.

"Next, be sure there is always sufficient nutritious, palatable, and economical food and drink readily available at all times. People get unpleasant if they're hungry or thirsty.

"Finally, take whatever your sound budget is and triple it. This music deserves to be heard, and people deserve to hear it the way it really is."

Ralph was not talking just about the bicentennial, he was talking about all kinds of festivals, because he believed that people are at their best when they are being entertained and cared for. He saw festivals as important and recurring celebrations, and into them he put all the basic principles that governed his work. He really used his principles; he built them into everything he ever did: inclusiveness, openheartedness, generosity, healthiness, concern with physical and mental program content, true care, real carefulness. It was really remarkable how he managed to realize most of his ideas in all his work.

It still surprises me that the Bicentennial Festival received so little notice in the newspapers and magazines of the time and that no one that I can track down has written a book about it. It should be better documented than I can do it here, and I would think that many people would like to try. But perhaps it was just too big, just too complex, just too three-four-five-six-dimensional to be explained on sheets of paper. And maybe that's all right. It was, and possibly should remain, one of a kind.

At the end of the last day of the 1976 festival, I walked along the Reflecting Pool from the Washington Monument down toward the Lincoln Memorial, putting the baby to bed. Already things looked a bit shabby: empty and silent, with papers blowing about the tents. A figure came toward me out of the dusk, a passionate Assyrian musician from San Francisco, and fell into step with me. After a bit he said, "Mrs. Hawes, when you begin to plan the next festival, make really sure that the pargos"—electric cars that roam festival grounds—"always give priority to musicians with large instruments." Although I knew of no future festival planning, I assured him that his concerns would be sympathetically handled, and we walked along together in the twilight as I marveled at the tenacity of human desires and the indestructibility of the human spirit.

My private and particular memory of the summer, though, was the Fourth of July—Independence Day—which was celebrated by a major opening-time hoo-ha down at the Lincoln Memorial. A crowd of important speakers was supposed to herald the occasion, and major press coverage was predicted. I had been to such affairs before, so I kept to my usual routine of festival program-visiting, starting at the less crowded end, the Regional America area, where that week the traditional arts of the southern states were being presented. I walked up to its outdoor stage and saw nobody on the stage or in the audience, but then I began to hear a thin piping and a couple of drums. I had heard this distinctive homemade music before on several Caribbean islands and in some southern states.

Then three black gentlemen, in their clean work clothes, walked in line out onto the big stage, one playing a battered bass drum, one a snare drum, and the third a cane fife that he had carved himself back in northern Mississippi, where they had played mostly at country dances. They had been at the festival several days, and I had heard them often. But this morning they looked incredibly like the *Spirit of '76*, and they were playing not their usual dance tunes but "The Battle Hymn of the Republic." They stood all by themselves on the big stage, and I sat all by myself in the empty audience seats with tears running down my face while they played—in good African American style—that grand old song over and over and over again until they decided it had been well and truly played. Then they marched back to the place where they had come from. I had been the only person to hear them, but I don't think they especially cared. And I sat there thinking: you know, the folks really always know what to do. I have never forgotten that.

ELEVEN

Moving to the National Endowment for the Arts

I ended the Bicentennial Festival with a number of strong impressions of great importance to me then and later:

- that an enormous number of Americans—far more than I had ever imagined—identified themselves on the most fundamental level as people belonging and beholden to a particular ethnicity, a particular occupation, a particular religion, a particular geographic region. Combinations of these elements also occurred, but people who didn't feel that they possessed at least one or two of these psychic hitching posts were really hard to find. And people tended to claim these smaller and perhaps more profound identities first—immediately followed by a statement of their equally firm attachment to the American nation, for which they felt a similarly fierce loyalty. One old Italian-born gentleman put it this way: "Italy is my mother; the United States is my wife."

- that a large number of these groups, although temporarily buoyed by the opportunity to display themselves at the festival, were in varying degrees of psychic pain. They felt that their history and their work—and therefore they themselves—had always somehow been overlooked and disrespected by mainstream intellectuals, by the business community, and by the various "big dogs" that had looked them over every now and again as possible sources of profit.

- that a serious intellectual schism divided almost every ethnic, religious, occupational, or regional group (not to mention the community of folklorists who were studying and working with them). One position held that the best survival stratagem for any small group was to identify with, make concessions to, try to infiltrate, and ultimately benefit in financial and power-positional terms from the majority culture. The opposing position held that the old-time stuff had lasted a long while and so was probably pretty good. Developed aesthetic systems should be defended on their own accounts, as creative and effective human responses to particular circumstances, thereby claiming their rightful places in the library of human inventions.

  The two stratagems sometimes alternate and sometimes even combine. We have, for example, the organized efforts of the South Carolina sweetgrass basket makers whose wares—including the winnowing baskets so essential in rice culture, as well as the woven cocktail trays with a sweetgrass circle holding each glass—are sold without comment by their makers along the highways leading into Charleston. Both ancient and modern designs are unmistakably produced by the same techniques and artistic principles.

  Even more impressive is the absorption of Delta Mississippi blues, Trinidadian calypso, Brazilian samba, and other local styles into the popular music business—not to mention the triumphant inventions of jazz and country music, brand-new musical creations now known all round the world.

- that strong, though rarely articulated, class distinctions continue looming in the background of *all* cultural activity in the United States.

Now I had to take these notions into a new setting. The Bicentennial Festival had come and gone, and, although I hung around the Smithsonian a bit helping clean things up, it was time for me to pack up and go back west. But then I got a phone call from the assistant director of the National Endowment for the Arts (NEA), Michael Straight, a friend of my brother's, inviting me to his office. So I went, and he asked me what I was planning to do now. I said that I was going back to California to resume my teaching at

CSUN, where they had held a place for me (I was by then a full professor with tenure). Mr. Straight offered me his hand and said, "Congratulations. With a secure job like that, what on earth would you want to stay on in Washington for?"

That seemed to be the end of the conversation, and I returned to my apartment feeling slightly mystified. But in a few days Nancy Hanks's office called. Ms. Hanks was at the time the NEA's director, a lady fabled throughout Washington for her energy, charm (especially featured in her meetings with southern congressmen), and blazing intelligence.

When I saw her, she offered me a job—after some ritual backings-and-forthings and one brisk fight—and at a very nice salary. In general terms, I gathered that I was to handle the problem of what the Endowment should do about folk arts. Our argument concerned her requirement that anyone in my proposed position must immediately fire a particular long-time staff member whom I knew, but whom she didn't like. I said that I wouldn't do that without a full fiscal year in which to help the staffer locate another suitable position, and I held my ground. I think Nancy rather liked my taking her on so directly; but from my point of view, I was still somewhat unsure whether I wanted to get into this agency or not, and she had gotten my Irish up a bit.

We finally agreed and shook on it, and on January 2, 1977, at 9:00 A.M., I walked into the National Endowment for the Arts as a new employee. I hadn't ever intended to do it, and in a million years I never thought I would stay in Washington so long. It was all pretty fuzzy as far as I was concerned, and although I had occasionally assisted as an outside panelist for the NEA Music Program in previous years, I had only the vaguest idea of what was to come.

When I walked through that front entrance, I inquired where, as a new employee, I should go. I was directed to a small private cubicle with a window and a door, a desk, a swivel chair, and a telephone. On the chair was a towering pile of miscellaneous papers, perhaps four feet tall. I asked my courteous guide what I was supposed to do, and he said, pointing to the pile, "Take care of that."

So I sat down, opened the first letter, and started to "take care of that" the best I could. By the end of the day I had determined what I minimally needed for this particular job, and I buttonholed my morning guide and said that I absolutely must have a typewriter, as well as a wall map of the United States. He said a typewriter was likely to be available, but he didn't know about the map. I told him that the map was probably more important than the typewriter, and that if he couldn't find one, I would.

The typewriter duly arrived, but not till several weeks later did my NEA friend confide in me that he had located a marvelous map of the USA, adding that it was simply too big. I said, "It can't possibly be too big—I want the biggest there is." And one glorious day, it arrived in my office, where it did indeed take up one entire wall. For the next fifteen years the adventures, setbacks, and successes of the Folk Arts Program were set out on this fabulous map—pierced to its vitals by multicolored pins—for all to see, especially me.

I cannot possibly explain how soothing, how stimulating, how consoling, how challenging it was for me to lie back in my chair at the end of every day and consider this brutally frank visual record of our puny attempts to see that all Americans got their chance to say their own special artistic say. We live in an enormous, incredible, and irreproducible country; I really knew so little of it, and there was so much to learn.

What I kept looking for (and sometimes found a hint of) was some kind of balance between the aesthetic reserves of an area and the fiscal, intellectual, and technical help available to enhance it. This balance could be, and generally was, totally skewed. I felt always we were dancing along cobwebs—and sometimes I thought that I was the only one in the dance who was beginning to learn that while money can sometimes lighten your steps, it sometimes can weigh you down. And at bottom, money was really our only tool.

Overall, I was enormously proud to be a federal employee. I believed I was acting as a go-between, helping negotiate the needs and desires of citizens as they wound their way through the complex structures of large government. And I had always been taught that government was the servant of the people, and that to clarify, formulate, and expedite the will of the people was an honorable activity that should require the sharpest intelligence and the widest experience.

It was sad that I began my government service during the Carter and Reagan anti-federal-bureaucracy campaigns. Several weeks after I had joined the NEA, I attended an evening party at the home of an "old Washington hand." I knew no one but my hosts there, but as I went down the formal receiving line, a well-dressed older gentleman asked me, "What do you do?" I said, with pride, that I had only just come to Washington to work at the National Endowment for the Arts. He said, with total and genuine disgust,

"Well, why don't you go back home to wherever it is you came from and see if you can't earn an honest living?"

I was aghast. It was so vicious, so unexpected, so undeserved, so personal—he really meant *me*. But I later heard many variations on that ugly theme during my Washington years, and in many ways it influenced my thinking and caused me to look more closely at the complex balance between federal, state, and private efforts.

My actual term of service at the National Endowment for the Arts began on January 2, 1977. It ended with my resignation on January 1, 1992. I served under Presidents Ford, Carter, Reagan, and the first Bush.

When I joined the NEA as what would nowadays be called a "public sector folklorist," I was certainly not being invited to trample across a previously unploughed field. The national fiddler's friend, Alan Jabbour, assisted by Claire Farrar, an anthropologist, had already been working there for years on folk arts projects proposed to the NEA long before I arrived on the Washington scene. When Alan quit the Endowment in 1976 to head the newborn American Folklife Center at the Library of Congress, he left behind a very useful working definition of the folk arts, as well as a record of participation in the granting process through the larger Endowment programs. Indeed, both before and after his departure, he and I had a collegial but vigorous argument as to just how the support of folk arts might or should develop within the Endowment.

As I've said, my office was a single small room. The work I did (and Alan's before me) flowed into a category of grant proposals for funding through the Special Projects Program, a larger unit where my office was situated. Special Projects was one of Nancy Hanks's good moves—a lively, flexible, not-very-big-money section where new ideas could develop, make their mistakes, grow, or decline in decent privacy. (If the ideas failed to jell, as they sometimes did, they had been, after all, only temporary projects, and little federal time or money had been lavished on them. In the private sector, such activities are often called "research and development.")

Special Projects regarded its new "folk folks" as the proper grant recipients for multiproject and multidiscipline events; these often turned out to be community festivals combining music, dance, storytelling. The program's time had been previously spent on strengthening and helping reshape proposals that might well have gone to begin with to one or the other of the major discipline programs: Theater, Literature, or Visual Arts, for example.

Alan Jabbour told me that he thought on balance that this was a healthy situation. "If we can keep attention on the traditional arts that are already spread out through the discipline programs," he told me, "they will be less vulnerable, less likely to get shot down, because nobody will know where to find them—they'll be all over the place." His thinking was that applications for the support of folk music should go to the Music Program, for folk theater to the Theater Program, for folk arts to the Visual Arts Program, and so on. I found less positive results from this situation.

The Music Program was one of the Endowment's biggest in terms of funding and influence, but under the remarkable, humane, and far-seeing leadership of its director, Walter Anderson, the program's staff had already been wrestling with the demands of nonstandard musics of all kinds—jazz, blues, traditional, ethnic, commercial, folk, and all points between. Indeed, in the heat of the battle Dr. Anderson titled one of the Music Program grant categories "Jazz/Folk/Ethnic."

Eventually, each discipline program director spoke to me directly and honestly of a deep concern for the root traditions from which they believed their particular discipline had sprung. I believed them; they wanted to fund their own traditional art forms and they knew they should. The problem inevitably turned out to be that the traditional art in question—initially always local, reflective of and appealing to a local audience—was often by most standards not truly competitive with the more complexly developed art forms.

To cite an example pulled together from several separate applications, the Endowment once received a request to help a tiny town in New Mexico provide new costumes for "Los Moros y Los Cristianos," a reenactment on horseback and in ancient Spanish of the bitter conflict between the Moors and the Christians in twelfth-century Spain. Perhaps five hundred local folks came to see the remains of this ancient drama annually; it had been presented in the same place every year for three centuries or so, and it was solidly *there*—probably the oldest theatrical presentation in the nation that we know of today. But over time the riders' cloaks and the horses' caparisons had become so worn you could hardly tell the Christians from the Moors, and the local community had no funds to buy the proper fabrics to replace them: the yards of gold braid, the essential fake rubies and pearls.

A savvy local priest suggested an appeal to the NEA grants office, which inspected the request and referred it to the Theater Program. The Theater Program nobly and correctly took it on, but in the final moments of the panel recommendations for the year, struggling with an inadequate budget . . . well, which way *should* a national agency's funding decision fall: for the urgent needs of a "Shakespeare in the Park" program, serving perhaps hundreds of thousands, or for the urgent needs of "Los Moros," with an audience of a fiftieth as many?

After observing several such impossible standoffs, I began to feel that only a separate, tradition-driven Folk Arts Program could hope to care for the variety of significant, local, traditional art forms that make our nation a mosaic of delight. Alan Jabbour, however, urged caution, suggesting a Brer Rabbit strategy (and there's nothing intrinsically wrong with that, by the way—hunkering down in the briar patch until sunnier times come around may often be the best solution).

I did see his point, but I also saw mine. New players can often accomplish feats impossible for the retiring side. And I was early pushed into looking at the potential field for a Folk Arts Program through two remarkably informative expeditions out of Washington.

Nancy Hanks liked her staff to get out in the field; she thought that that was where the action was and she was certainly right, at least for me. And she insisted on immediate reports when a staffer returned. All such documents would be found returned on one's desk the following morning, complete with marginal notes from Miss Hanks (an example of personal industry and administrative attentiveness I have never seen equaled).

My first two major ventures into the outer world were to the state of Maine and, later, to Atlanta, Georgia. I was actually invited first by the Maine Arts Council—what a thrill, somebody really wanted me! When I got off the plane in Bangor, I learned that the executive director of the Maine Arts Council had just been hospitalized with a broken leg. He had therefore assigned my already planned three-day tour to an assistant, who nobly struggled for days to introduce me to Maine local arts (maybe traditional? maybe folk? maybe pop? maybe idiosyncratic? what on earth *were* they anyway?) in ways that would fit within overall national program definitions. Neither he nor I was ever exactly sure what we were talking about, but we really tried at least to see a sample of what was going on in Maine. We packed that trip really full—I was not going to let one unnecessary single federal dollar get past my hand.

As we drove out of Bangor headed into central Maine, my courteous and hardworking young host commented that I might not realize that I was the very first national program director from the Endowment ever to visit Maine. I found this astonishing—how on earth could that be? But we charged on into two days of a marvelous and confusing sort of hodgepodge: a tour of stained glass windows installed on house fronts all through one small city, all made by the first glass-blowing company in the state back in the late 1800s; several lively central European ethnic choruses, as well as an enormous, well-trained mandolin orchestra; a college-based glee club singing sea chanteys and fisherman's ballads; a couple of local coffeehouses with entertainment; and far too many small-town museums pining away from lack of money and sporting mostly local relics all the way from housewife diaries to grandpa's old farm implements—all of the foregoing conceived, developed, and enthusiastically supported by local citizens and/or arts councils.

Indeed, as we headed into the potato fields that stretched all the way to the Canadian border, we were joined by the vigorous director of the Aroostook County Arts Council, who remarked cheerfully that she wanted a good chance to talk with the state council man (my chauffeur and guide) because this was the very first time anybody from the Maine state arts agency had ever visited Aroostook County and she had a lot to say. I refrained from comment. Later on the conversation became more general and produced the interesting information that all state workers had been advised not to visit Maine Indian reservations temporarily until a few unfortunate disagreements over some culturally insensitive new regulations had been resolved. So I couldn't go either (it was probably just as well—I was quite unprepared).

My Maine trip ended with a stopover at a brave and adventurous project: the Acadian Village in Van Buren. Passionate and dedicated workers had already moved several large period structures to the proposed site and were busily making them visitable. I spent a whole afternoon looking things over and conferring about financing, what further expertise was needed, and fundraising methods. That evening, the entire Van Buren population (it seemed to me) attended a dinner party and dance held in my honor in the recently moved local schoolhouse. It was the merriest of affairs, featuring live music and excellent Acadian food and drink, the whole evening capped by my overhearing a comment from the Acadian Village director to the local Aroostook County council representative: "You know, my dear, I am especially delighted to see you because this is the very first time anybody from the Aroostook County Arts Council ever visited up here!" None of these people had been in touch before.

I flew home from Maine with a lot to think about, including the unexpected effects of outsider visits toward the stimulation of sociability and new perspectives, as well as the enormous variation between what many citizens assumed were folk arts and my own assumptions.

But I'd guess the most influential, mind-bending, and long-lasting impression I took home from Maine was that *everybody* felt somehow vaguely neglected and unappreciated. This included not only the Indians, but the odd ethnic choir, and the local historical or arts society—in a word, everybody really. In later years I was to extend this perception to the entire population of the United States. Somehow in our democratic society every single citizen seems to feel at bottom undervalued, unrequited.

Responding to this unspoken angst, I believe, was the secret of Eleanor Roosevelt's success on the road. She simply honestly admired the constructive elements of the local people's activities, and she said so loud and clear. Before her, nobody had really gotten around to voicing such approval, or at least the local people felt that they hadn't. I was enormously flattered to be told by an old Maine lady that I reminded her of Eleanor Roosevelt's long ago visit.

Georgia turned out to be *very* different, although just as educational a trip. In honor of the new president, Jimmy Carter, a groundbreaking exhibition of southern arts and crafts from quilting to furniture making had been mounted at the Atlanta Museum. It was titled Missing Pieces, and it consisted of exquisite examples of southern craftsmanship. I was invited down, along with other NEA program directors, to attend the opening festivities, and we enjoyed the warm hospitality and instant familiarity granted us by our southern hosts and hostesses. As part southerner myself—I am Texas-born—I appreciated every nuance.

During my two-day visit I was invited to address the state arts council. I blithely assumed that its failure to fund many of Georgia's traditional artists was just because its members hadn't yet realized the cultural significance of their activities. I got straightened around quickly. After I had extolled the capacities for music education to be discovered in the remarkable theories of Bessie Jones, the superb African American singer of St. Simons Island, I was gently informed by a council lady that I should be aware that everybody had had mammies who had sung to them, but what the arts council wanted to know was how to get those little black children to play the violin. Later an elderly gentleman quietly told me during a coffee break, "You know what we call an expert around here? He's a son-of-a-bitch from out of town."

I believed then and now that these interactions were not intended as insulting or angry (although I must admit there was a strong element of pointing out to a young southern woman where she was going astray in her thinking). Essentially, though, they were attempts to make clear to me how they believed their particular artistic world worked. They failed.

A more productive and also highly educational occasion during my Atlanta trip was a joyful meeting with a brilliant young educator who had developed an enormously popular and effective curriculum for motivating young Appalachian teenagers to continue their education. He regularly assigned all his students to interview senior residents in their own hometowns concerning how they had lived during the "early days," concentrating on how they built, crafted, cooked, trapped, slaughtered, and stored—all the old-timey essential rural life skills. These individual interviews were then edited into book form and printed, along with diagrams, maps, and photographs, in an actual book series written, produced, and marketed through the efforts of the students themselves. It was a truly fascinating and complex procedure.

The *Foxfire* paperback series came along during the folksong revival period and proved tremendously successful, appealing not only to senior citizens themselves, but also to those of the younger generation who loved to imagine themselves returning to simpler and "more real" ways of living. Sales were huge, and while I was in Atlanta I myself picked up several volumes (I had never read any before, although I had often heard of the project).

But reading the work itself on the plane home, I became uneasy about the whole idea. It took me a while, but I finally had to admit to myself that the books actually bored me. The interviews were mostly routine and superficial accounts of meetings that surely must have been livelier and more interesting. They also didn't sound, in many places, quite right to me—some of the methodologies described didn't seem really accurate or even possible. I began to wonder if many of the seniors being interviewed hadn't thought they were just helping out the youngsters with a school assignment, without giving it their full adult attention. Where was the humor, the richness, or the imagery I believed must have been there? And then I got the pesky notion that perhaps to be interviewed by unknown children might seem to some old-timers a waste of their time and maybe even a tad insulting. I began to feel such projects were clearly educationally sound, but folklorically and artistically weak. This was to be my first, but not my last, confrontation with the multiple complexities of introducing folk arts into an educational curriculum. So many people seemed to take it for granted that folk ways are "childish" and therefore "good for children."

Venturing into Maine and Georgia together made me realize that I must increase my understanding of the agency in which I was working. I did not then look into the history of the National Endowment for the Arts—I never had time. But some fundamental things gradually became clear. The agency came into being because of the economic and political clout of what one might call the upper-class arts world: the symphony associations, the opera guilds, and the ballet and art museum boards. These groups were wealthy and, naturally, set up a system that fed into the support of their particular view of the world of the arts. Their arts were truly big-time. For example, in order to qualify for some NEA high-culture categories, an applying group had to be able to specify that its operating budget was at least at the six-figure level. Other and smaller programs offered fellowships to individual artists who, by applying, entered into competition with all the other novelists, photographers, poets, sculptors, or painters who cared to try from across the entire nation.

Neither funding pattern seemed suitable for traditional arts or artists, but it gradually became clear to me that any incipient Folk Arts Program would be—like it or not—working within a system that had been set up to help support the needs of such international icons as the Metropolitan Museum of Art, the Chicago Symphony, Rudolf Nureyev, and Yo-Yo Ma. It was a bit daunting. I pulled up my socks and decided to go after what I truly believed and what I most wanted to demonstrate: that the peak of achievement in every aesthetic system was worthy of the same respect. But there were so many widespread misconceptions that had to be addressed almost everywhere.

TWELVE

Creating the Folk Arts Program

First of all, any fledgling Folk Arts Program had to wade through the usual thicket of misconceptions about the folk arts themselves. Even at the National Endowment for the Arts, the most unassailable of these was and is the widespread notion that the singular function of traditional aesthetic systems is just to hang around for a while, being a stable bedrock and providing nutrients for the growth of later complexities, later styles, and later inventions.

I hope I don't seem querulous or unappreciative here; my devotion to the extraordinary staff of the NEA is intense. It's just that they too, like me, were brought up in the middle-class American cultural surround, subject in varying degrees to the middle-class American ideas of what's good and what's laughable.

For I found that there was an ever-present comic miasma hanging about the whole idea of the folk arts—an insidious, creeping, straw-hatted, "Oy veh," "Wall, I swan" déclassé stereotype. My friend the folklorist Barre Toelken used to identify this image as "dancing with your elbows out." Many people consider this sort of thing simply part of some "country yokel" or "Amos and Andy" act, humorous but affectionate. It can be affectionate, of course; everyday folks enjoy and appreciate corn just as much as anybody else.

More sober Endowment staff were always commenting about the roars of laughter that came out of the Folk Arts Program—it was, indeed, a merry place to work. But we also knew that much of our material was simultaneously funny and deadly serious, and that serious problems were often being presented to us.

By contrast, it also appeared that the Folk Arts Program was somehow tapping into the tender and emotional feelings of those people in and out of the Endowment who were the strongest supporters of justice, fair play, and equal rights. Here a deep concern seemed to express itself in comments that the "little" folk arts were willy-nilly being ground to bits under the chariot wheels of oncoming complex cultures.

And so they often were, of course. A native speaker from an Alaskan tribe told Barre Toelken that her children had been whipped for speaking their native language on the school playground. "Maybe you've turned it around now," she told him, "but I don't really know if you have, so *I don't teach nobody nothing*—no language, no songs, no nothing. I don't want no more kids to suffer."

Such stories got heard both by the Endowment and by general arts audiences. And when I described those situations in my own talks, lots of people cried (and sometimes I did too). It wasn't phony, it was all real—and when you heard it for the two-hundredth time from the two-hundredth group, it was a large-scale human tragedy. But after a while I began to feel that simply getting people to feel sad about endangered skills, arts, languages, or whatever maybe wasn't terribly useful and might even suggest that everything was already lost anyhow. Such general lamentations could well be taking possible supporters off the hook: if the traditional arts were so far gone, perhaps heroic efforts to save them were irrelevant.

Examining our overall program, I had to admit that, with the best of intentions, the Endowment's Folk Arts Program was dangerously close to presenting the folk arts as ancient, feeble, and moribund, or—contrariwise— countrified, sentimental, and/or comical.

Now this wasn't fair, and it just wouldn't do. I laid down a rule for myself and, hopefully, all who might follow me: from this day forth (I decreed to myself and anyone else who would hold still) no federal public expression, written or verbal, should allow the folk arts of America or any other part of the world to be portrayed as either comical or pitiful. They should be spoken of as sentient, strong, and intimately keyed into the essential structures of their own particular cultures. The not-even-quite-there Folk Arts

Program began to announce that the Endowment would support only the very best traditional products of any culture that was in active existence in the United States. Our recommendations for support of Eskimo or Hawaiian dance festivals were aesthetically just as crucial as the Dance Program's recommendations for the support of classical ballet tours, and that was to be our official stance for the entire program for the foreseeable future.

For we had very quietly become an official NEA program. Almost nobody was looking at the time, except a few Endowment stalwarts, a very few folklorists, and the recently retired Nancy Hanks. But it was a major step. The overall Endowment was just then enjoying great public support; it was expanding, even booming, and arts across the nation were being celebrated. It was a generous and expansive time, and the proposed Folk Arts Program managed to slip through the opening door and become part of the celebration. It is important to be ever sensitive and alert to such possibilities—it may be a long time before others come along. I used to amuse myself by remembering Kurt Vonnegut's brilliant suggestion that there was always a magical moment (at least in all monetary transactions) when the substance involved belonged to no one—neither seller nor buyer—and it was during those split seconds that a third party might be able to slip in and take it. He believed such clever, thieving brigands to be mostly lawyers, but the Folk Arts Program managed the same maneuver a few times too.

In order to secure our position, however, we had to clarify the confusion as to the nature and essence of the folk arts. In fact during my first year at the Endowment I felt that every person I met was tacitly saying, "Well, I'm delighted to meet you because I am sure you can straighten out for me just what *are* the folk arts anyway?" The following is a summary of what I generally wound up saying (although I hope I said it more briefly).

Let's just break it down a bit. *Art* can be defined as expressive behavior that reaches us in a multitude of forms—for example, dance, song, tale, painting, sculpture, design. And it always shows, beyond its overt content, one or more crucial secondary meanings. That isn't the greatest definition in the world, but it's enough to go on with.

Folk (I would then say) is an old-fashioned term for social group—especially for people who share such important characteristics as religion, occupation, geographic location, language, and so on. Most of us actually identify ourselves by listing several of the "folk" groups to which we believe we do or do not belong: "Well, I'm from south New Jersey and my parents came over from Poland back in the forties, and I work in the power plant.

My wife is Catholic, but I don't pay too much attention to all that, and my kids go to Sunday school and Saturday school too so they can talk with their Jewish grandparents." This person represents at least seven folk groups, all of which have their own artistic expression—their own folklore.

Most people actually do belong to more than one folk group and thus have experienced several folk arts already, for it turns out that every folk group has invented its own particular identifying artistic repertoire and characteristic style. Indeed the first thing a tradition seems to do is to put its best (self-identifying) foot forward by informally developing particular signals, jokes, special languages, signs, a repertoire of songs, stories, games, whatever is appropriate for making plain just where this particular culture fits in.

Different folk groups, of course, differ and have differed in the creativity and intensity they invest in particular artistic traditions. For example, some, like East Coast African Americans, seem to have put an enormous amount of creative energy into music (as well as other things such as storytelling), while others, like southwestern Native Americans, have intensely developed their visual arts. Such qualities emerge, thrive, subside, and change according to the needs and interests of the particular group, as well as other factors.

And that's why it's hard to give a simple and universally comprehensible definition of the term "folk arts." It is made of the particular aesthetic traditions that one simply knows about because one grows up in a given culture area at a given time. And though fortunate people are deeply aware of how complex their music is, how elegant their dancing, their carving, their costumery are, they may at the very same time believe them old-fashioned and out of date and even somewhat embarrassing.

This is partly because of the gradual change in a formerly established generational pattern. Children tend to learn their traditional culture from the grandparental generation, which teaches a host of skills, attitudes, and responsibilities to the child while the parental generation is busy making a living. Later, the responsibilities shift up the line: when the children become parents and a third generation appears, the parents become grandparents. It's a sort of interlocking chain, and it has worked for centuries and is still powerful. I believe it's worth fighting for—at least against the current possibility of a world where the old folks spend their days in retirement homes and the kids spend theirs in day care or video arcades.

Then another question arises: if the folk arts are generally picked up along one's way from earlier generations, without requiring formal instruction and in everyday settings (back porches, town squares, and the like), why do such informal processes need money, most especially money from the federal government? And where could such money and national effort actually be both needed and effective?

The folk arts may be just going along in their mostly quiet pattern doing their own local or regional thing, but as time goes by they find they are up against blindingly strong competition from the national communication systems, as well as from the national educational systems—both of which are wealthy, powerful, and extremely resistant to fundamental change. Both are also totally committed to the ascendancy of the classical and popular arts of the Western world over every other aesthetic system, not excepting the folk arts.

With good reason, the American people are proud of their overarching educational and communication systems. They broadcast, far and wide, an enormous amount of vital information; they oppose illiteracy with rhetoric, care, and hard cash; they trumpet a democratic capacity for mitigation and change; they expose the excitement of inventiveness all around the world. But they are frequently so loud and so brazen and so indebted to private gain that they drown out softer, smaller, but equally important and yeasty local voices.

It is almost impossible to exaggerate the impact of contemporary radio, television, tape recordings, and their dazzling paraphernalia of contemporary hardware upon the small communities in which they also appear. In the Micronesian islands I visited in the 1980s, I heard family radios blaring from every bamboo hut as well as every concrete building. They were keeping their audiences abreast of local weather conditions, anticipated ship and sailing canoe schedules, special messages for crew members, and projected arrival times. This information was not casual; it was often crucial and no one could afford to miss it.

But what I also heard, between the informational announcements, throughout the small islands of Micronesia, was a nearly continuous blast of third-rate American disco music and semi-military American high school bands. I was informed when I reached home that many local radio stations in the mainland United States made "charitable" contributions of their out-of-date or otherwise useless discs to local Pacific broadcasters.

It seemed a tragically wasted opportunity. Why couldn't the sounds of *local* musics and those of the other Pacific islands, as well as the *greatest* of the popular music of the United States, as well as the classical musics of the world, fill the shady green dirt roads of the Pacific islands? I spoke with a number of people about this on my return. No one was really interested; it was too small or too big, perhaps too intellectual or too do-goody an idea. Mostly, I fear, there was no obviously profitable reason to go to all that trouble, no way of getting any of the money back.

My mother knew a great many proverbs and spread them liberally before her children. One was the widespread "He who has, gets," and that one returned to my recollection often during my NEA years. Perhaps a federal program like Folk Arts should concentrate only on the federal-sized problems that neither private agencies nor local communities may ever be in shape to tackle. But we didn't have enough money to get into that bigger game, so I put aside the notion of a collection of music of the world's people set up especially for local radio stations for a while. The right time might come along, sooner or later or someday.

⌒

When I first undertook the Endowment job, my brother Alan—seven years my senior and twenty-six years more experienced in the interaction of folklore, academia, and politics—told me something that, in many subtle ways, forever shaped the principles and policies that the Folk Arts Program eventually forwarded. It was a typical Alan Lomax remark: unexpected, outrageous, half sincere, half joking, at bottom profound. He said, "Bess, I have come to believe that God invented folklorists and set them here on this planet simply to ensure that by no possible accident or procedural quirk will *any* of the folks get *any* of the money."

Hardly a day passed in my Endowment tenure that I didn't think of that. It turned out to be the most troublesome aspect of the job I held for fifteen years: how to get any of the money past the long line of intermediary figures, including the many noble bureaucrats such as me. (I was pulling down a pretty good salary during those years.)

During the late 1960s and early 1970s a huge campaign had developed for the establishment of a federally located American Folk Center. Serious efforts to lobby for such a bill were organized by thousands of voters including, among others, my brother Alan, my great friend Ralph Rinzler, and my favorite occasional sparring partner Archie Green, whose value as a professional folklorist, consistently available to walk the congressional halls and press the flesh and tell the good stories, was inestimable.

Since the demise in 1943 of the Works Progress Administration, Congress had entertained a variety of plans to initiate other efforts in the arts and humanities. WPA programs had been based on the truly remarkable thesis that unemployed housepainters might be paid a modest living wage by the government for painting houses that needed to be painted, and thus musicians might put bread on the family table by playing their instruments for people who wanted to listen—this in place of any kind of universal government dole or some variety of conscripted labor. The searching and anxious debate over how to replace or even improve the old WPA programs had brought issues of content, community control, and public access to the arts into discussion. The then unfamiliar system of grants-in-aid was beginning to burgeon as well.

All this serious discussion had raised the level of debate, and at one point there was indeed a plan to initiate three separate cooperative federal funding entities: humanities, arts, and traditional (folk) arts. This eminently sensible structure came within a whisker of being put into effect; unfortunately, it ran into a turf war between the already established federal cultural agencies and sank to rise no more.

During the early period of congressional attention, Livingston Biddle (at the time legislative assistant to Senator Claiborne Pell of Rhode Island) was in charge of drafting the establishing legislation for the support of the arts and the humanities. One day he was informed that a Miss Sarah Gertrude Knott of the National Folk Festival wished to see him. He agreed to see her, and a lady in white gloves, a dark suit, and a pouffed Gibson Girl hairdo capped by a summer straw hat topped with a feathered bird sailed (Livvy said there was no other verb to describe it) into his office, her pennants streaming. When he inquired what he could possibly do for such a formidable figure, she replied that she had observed that the definition of "art" in proposed NEA legislation listed many art forms, but not folk arts. Miss Knott had come to ensure that the arts of the American people were included in all upcoming legislation. She said to Mr. Biddle that "folk arts" *must* be listed along with sculpture, opera, dance, and literature as important parts of American aesthetic production. And such was her assurance of total rightness that Mr. Biddle (having responded, as he told me later, "Yes, ma'am") set forth to do just that.

The world of politics is simultaneously permeable and impermeable. One must never stop trying to get through, because the cracks allowing access come up in the most extraordinary places at the weirdest times. Miss Knott's expedition into Senator Pell's O. K. Corral had a result I doubt that anyone could have anticipated. Folk arts were forever thereafter routinely mentioned in the NEA's authorizing legislation as a part of the definition of art; and as a result, the agency was *legally required* to do something about them. Even when the far superior notion of the three cooperating funding agencies had crashed, Gertrude Knott's and Livingston Biddle's insertion of the two words "folk arts" into the Arts Endowment's legislation continued to have an enormous effect.

We can see the reverse of this in examining the National Endowment for the Humanities (NEH), which I believe Miss Knott ignored or downplayed (perhaps because of her particular interest in traditional performance rather than scholarship). The NEH had organized itself into a functional, rather than disciplinary, structure; for example, an application for archaeological research into the off-shore California islands might well be reviewed by one mixed body of scholars to ascertain the professional qualifications of the proposed research staff, by another to examine the research methodologies designed for the project, and later by experts qualified to determine its overall importance in terms of the current needs of the American archaeology— three different judging groups working from three different perspectives. This was a difficult obstacle course for a traditional group such as a tribe or an ethnic community, and although some fine folklore projects were funded by NEH, others were criticized as being academic and self-referential, re-quiring enormous labor for every application.

One morning during my Smithsonian stint Ralph Rinzler descended into my office, plucked me from my desk in that whirlwind style that was ever his gift, and whisked me by cab to the Capitol and therein to what must have been one of those sinister locations known as a Capitol "back room."

Actually, it was just a miscellaneous sort of room with some miscellaneous people sitting around a long table under rows of gloomy oil paintings. Ar-chie Green, I remember, was there, perhaps Alan Jabbour (I am not sure), several "old Washington hands," and two or three congressional political aides. There were lots of yellow legal-size pads on the table and lots was being written on them. As I watched my confreres at work, myself still con-fused, it suddenly hit me: My God, what we're doing here is writing a bill! The Congress of the United States may actually give these miscellaneous scribbles their serious consideration.

Is this the way it really happens: a few scattered people with mutual inter-ests gathering together on a Wednesday afternoon to work up propositions that could possibly affect people across the United States for generations?

I kept thinking that nobody had ever said that it was even all right for us to do this—and then asking myself, well, who could? We were just doing it. Could this miscellaneous group of people, including *me*, actually know what to do about the problems facing *the Congress of the United States?*

Of course, that was and is essentially the way our government both does and does not work, and I only later began to realize the glory of it. Throughout my federal experience of about twenty years, although I objected to many particular federal actions, I increasingly came to admire the structures behind it. We do not always realize, I think, what a fortunate people we are.

For only one example, I discovered that every single program in every federal agency appears once a year before two congressional committees— one from the House and one from the Senate—for a brisk and often penetrating review of its budgetary needs. During my tenure, the Arts Endowment was fortunate to have the Honorable Sidney Yates of Chicago as chairman of our House review committee. He was superb: informed, urbane, witty, thorough. Our hearings before Congressman Yates were always in the months of April or May, and they always seemed to me to function (at least for the Folk Arts Program) like an old-fashioned spring cleaning. When we were done, I felt better: fresh, new, and ready to start a new year.

My first appearance before Congressman Yates was in 1977 when the Folk Arts Program had barely gotten started, had no money to speak of, and was still trying to convince the larger arts world that we had something to offer. I went up to the big conference table feeling nervous, not to say wobbly, but Congressman Yates asked me in the friendliest way, "Well, you're new, aren't you? How're you doing?" And I found myself saying, "Well, Congressman, Folk Arts is doing just about the way an old-time black spiritual put it: we're inching along just like a poor inch worm."

"Why, Bess Hawes," he said, "I'm surprised at you. I thought you'd be quoting one of the great old British ballads like 'I'm struck, I'm struck, His Lordship said, I'm struck, but I'm not slain. I'll just lie down and bleed a while, and rise to fight again!'"

Now a fellow who can quote a traditional British ballad offhand is a fellow you want to testify before. And each following year after a brief relaxing chat—which he always started by inquiring "How's your brother Alan?"—Congressman Yates and I got down to business, taking a thorough look-see into every corner of the Folk Arts operation.

I always wished we had had a bit more time at the hearings because, bless him, Yates was such a devotee of the European-based fine arts that he was always a bit doubtful, I believe, about the actual work that the Folk Arts Program was undertaking—not doubtful of me, but of the art itself. He never got a chance to experience the people's art at its best, but like a good democrat/Democrat he believed that everybody should somehow get into the action and this was probably a good way to do it, so he would support it to the end. Besides, he knew of my father's and brother's work at the Library of Congress, and I believe he was personally pleased to see yet another experienced family member devoted to governmental service.

Between congressional hearings it was rare for any senator or representative to pressure the Folk Arts Program, requesting special consideration for any of their constituents. Partly this was due to the fact that our available funds were so small as to be unattractive to the kind of big-time cultural operation that wanted to show its potential federal "muscle." Partly it was the clear message we continually broadcast that our program had plain and specified rules and limitations that could be reexamined and corrected, but not casually violated for someone's temporary convenience. We took our guidelines seriously and insisted that others do so too.

At the same time, if we could not serve an applicant directly, we believed we should try our best to be of assistance to this citizen, and we sent out letter after letter and spent hour after hour on the phone suggesting where the desired project might better fit or how it might accommodate itself to certain guidelines without destroying its integrity. Our overall belief that the federal government is the servant of the people led the amazing staff of the Folk Arts Program ever onward in an impossible and vain but still glorious intention to help, or at least to give solace to everyone who came to us. I got to be terribly proud of the staff and how they did their jobs.

Such conversations we all had! When I passed our intrepid grants officer's cubicle it was in no way unusual for me to hear her say, "All right, Mrs. _____, let's get out another big piece of paper, and let's draw a line right down through the middle. And on one side we'll list every single thing you need so as to put up your Hmong embroidery exhibition the way it ought to be, and on the other we'll put down whether you already have it and how much it would cost if you had to buy it . . ."

For many of our applicants were sending in their first-ever grant proposals. Their concept (if they had one) of "soft match" was fuzzy, since many had never considered that they were already making a contribution to their project in ways that could be estimated in monetary terms (available space, materials, equipment usage, donated labor, and so on). I came to feel that perhaps one of our important contributions was to provide, for innocent emerging groups, a delicate though positive introduction into the world of budgets and fiscal responsibility. I wasn't so good at it myself (in my own life, so far, I have never yet applied for a grant) and so had lots of sympathy for newcomers who had never ever thought, for example, of applying for nonprofit status, since making a profit was so completely out of the range of possibility it had never occurred to them to try.

I also spoke often with westerners, mid- and far, who had built-in suspicions of *any* federal effort, especially money-based, and didn't want ever to get involved with "the government." And I found myself saying irritably on more than one occasion, "All right, Mr. _____, you've probably sent Washington a lot of tax money and you've fussed about it. Now here's a good chance to say what you personally think ought to be done with it. Should we mail it back to your county or state agencies to help them send that fine old saddle maker and rawhide braider around to teach some of the local kids in the public schools? Or would you rather we contribute it to buy another couple of clamps for the next stealth bomber? It's your money, not ours."

Actually, this kind of conversation led to my favorite part of the entire interchange. The way we played it, there eventually had to be a negotiation between the applicants and the Folk Arts Program. They brought what they had to contribute (mostly art) and we brought what we had (mostly money) and, in one way or another, we put all of it on the table. If we were lucky, there was an intervening state or local folk arts coordinator who could help clarify the interaction. But almost always, although it was sometimes complicated or even passionate, there was a dignified exchange during which hardly any tribal or community leader, I believe, felt diminished or pushed about.

At the same time, I continually wondered if the best use of the Folk Arts Program's powers was really to instruct tribes, unions, brotherhoods, urban organizations, and ethnic groups in how to fill out various governmental forms—a rather pitiful goal, after all. Point for point, I never really ever decided what exactly should have been done, although I notice I tended to favor the strategies I myself knew best how to handle. Perhaps that is always the way we go on, really, doing what we can as and when we can.

THIRTEEN

Guidelines, Panels, and Policies

Every morning I was greeted by a brand-new pile of what I always secretly thought of as "this" (remembering my first day at NEA). "This" invariably turned out to be a glorious mishmash, containing such items as letters of sober inquiry from mammoth universities for mammoth research projects requiring mammoth amounts of money (often several times the Folk Arts Program's annual budget), requests for support from individual folksong "composers" or folksong arrangers, monies to start up publishing or performance projects, applications for any available loose cash from desperate small arts agencies (forwarded to us by equally desperate local or state grants officers), as well as a multitude of charming or belligerent proposals from the nation's ever-hopeful loonies. And then there were the serious ones who just didn't know very much except what they thought ought to happen. Every day the twice-a-day stack of mail and the drop-in visitors focused me on the horrendous puzzle of how on earth the United States government (embodied momentarily in me and my cohorts) should respond to the cultural concerns of this complex citizenry anyway. And I was not the only staffer so engaged.

One night in 1990 Dan Sheehy, assistant director of the Folk Arts Program, suffered a severe attack of insomnia. Next morning he told us he had tried to overcome it with all the usual mental gymnastics and finally arranged himself a mental map of the United States, filling in all the various cultural groups that had ever consulted us (thereby counting "ethnicities," so to speak, instead of sheep). He started on the West Coast and proceeded slowly across the country, moving from north to south by regions. By the time he was partway across, he had gotten so fascinated that he got out of bed and wrote it all down on his computer, stayed up the rest of the night, and handed me the results in the following document, along with the comment that he would bet that between the two of us we could remember each one of the following groups and their projects. (And it turned out we nearly could.)

August 1, 1990

To whom it may interest:

This is the totally unscientifically ascertained list of the "cultural groups" or "ethnicities," as they identified themselves to us, with whom I can remember having worked at the Arts Endowment over the years. I count 91 in all.

Dan

Afro-Puerto Rican	Albanian	Anglo
Apache	Arapaho	Ashkenazi
Athabascan	Basque	Blackfoot
Bulgarian	Cahuilla	Calabrian
Cherokee	Cheyenne	Chumash
Colesville Tribe	Comanche	Cree
Crow	Crucian (St. Croix)	Cupa
Czech	Dakota Sioux	Dalmatian
Danish	Delaware	Dieguenos
Dutch	Finnish	French
German	Greek	Gros Ventre
Haida	Hawaiian	Hispanic Puerto Rican
Hoopa	Hopi	Inupiaq
Irish	Iroquois	Italian
Kiowa	Klickitat	Laguna Pueblo
Lakota Sioux	Lumbee	Lummi
Macedonian	Maidu	Makah

Mesquokie	Minorcan	Mitchif
Miwok	Navajo	Nez Perce
Nooksack	Norwegian	Oglala Sioux
Ojibwa	Oneida	Paiute
Polish	Pomo	Pontic Greek
Port Gamble Salish	Portuguese	Rumanian
Rumanian/Jewish	Samish	Scottish
Seminole	Sephardic	Shoshone
Shoshone-Bannock	Skokomish	Slovenian
Spanish	Swedish	Tlingit
Tohono O'odham	Tolowa	Tsimshiam
Turkish	Ukrainian	Ute
Yaqui	Yokut (near Fresno)	Yurok
Zuni		

And there were still more to come. There was no possible way any small office such as ours could properly assist such a range of emotionally charged folks. We just didn't know enough to cope with all this, and we realized we never would. For a while, in consultation with the Library of Congress Folklife Center, we tried to work out a battery of expert advisers to help us in each state, but we soon realized that we just couldn't do it. We had neither the time nor the resources to set up the job the way we knew it should be done, so we just went on day by day, consulting with the experts we knew or learned of, handling things the best way we could see. It was all a little bit catch-as-catch-can, but in the process of all this thinking I began to consider how we might strengthen our own position. And in the process of working out reasonably appropriate answers to our multi-needy clientele—answers that wouldn't forever embarrass either them or the program—I began to face the power and the importance of the guideline.

Guidelines announce in advance what you believe you can do and what you probably can't do. Such a marvelous invention could possibly serve to focus attention quickly on the folk or traditional materials that best fit our congressional mandate. And a set of well-composed, tightly formulated guidelines might also keep us from becoming a sort of ultimate wastebasket for creative products and activities that didn't fit anywhere else.

The Folk Arts staff, aided by its early panels, determined that our guidelines should contain a rigorous, but understandable, description/definition of the nature of the traditional arts, along with a detailing of at least a number of ways by which such arts might be energized or benefited. We also announced that program support (bureaucratese for the money) would go to those applications that strengthened the traditional art in itself, for itself, as it lay and where it lay, rather than supporting outside artists learning or utilizing the art. For example, a composer's sumptuous arrangement for symphony orchestra of a traditional Appalachian melody was defined as outside the domain of the Folk Arts Program, since the result would likely have spoken to and benefited the symphony-going audience more than the original singers or their own audiences. Such proposals to "fix up" the folk arts for outsider appreciation would be referred by Folk Arts to the Music Program with our blessings (which were often quite sincere).

The Folk Arts Program's first guidelines (1978) established a publication pattern to which we tried to hold. Added to the normal application, we produced a breast-pocket, purse-sized folder written in everyday English (sometimes Spanish), profusely illustrated with photographs of Yiddish dancers, western saddle makers, Polish egg-dyers, black quartets, and others. Our aim was always to create a federal document the intention of which could be understood by an ordinary citizen without resort to a lawyer, a dictionary, or an interpreter. Our guidelines worked pretty well, needed little revising in later years, and were interesting to read—and I still feel proud of them.

Clearly, right from the beginning we tried to establish a delicate balance between rigidity and openness in such federal initiatives as ours. I have since thought that the working out of this yin/yang principle may in part be responsible for the success of certain projects and the collapse of others. Maybe, to give one small example, there *has* to be a firm structure within which improvisation *can* take place—a powerful, but constricted, surround filled with relaxed elements to be enjoyed and released at later times. Overall, complementarity is essential. There must be some sort of balance, although there are many possible relationships I suppose.

In the Folk Arts Program, without particularly intending to do so, our guidelines wound up being severe in the area of *what* folk arts were, and relaxed about *who* got to do interesting things with them (as long as the traditional artists retained aesthetic rights). Our neighbors in the Expansion Arts Program took exactly the opposite stratagem: they didn't care nearly so much *what* was done as *who* got to do it, their fundamental concern being the development of minority artists, arts agents, and agencies. One of the many remarkable achievements of the NEA always seemed to me the collegial reciprocity of the Folk Arts and Expansion Arts Programs: neither could have truly succeeded without the other. Both were critically important, and both still have critically useful issues to resolve between the two approaches. And, somehow or other, we kept on staggering along together.

I myself began to recognize three important things:

1. Guidelines do not leap from bureaucrats' or artists' brows. They emerge from many sources and then work their way through layer upon layer of legal and customary regulations, including scrutiny by the august National Council on the Arts, the advisory body appointed by the president of the United States to make final recommendations on all applications for any kind of arts funding.

2. Although guidelines must be used to announce the actual state of a program's way of doing things, there is nothing to prevent the inclusion at any time of suggestions or hints of how things *might* be going to be done in future. Such formulas as "the program would be interested in projects addressing . . ." or "projects involving new developments in (whatever) are of special interest" may fairly signal future, as well as present, emphases. All guidelines should be read carefully—they have not been jotted down quickly.

3. If some kind of serious change in a federal program's direction is being proposed, a minimum of three years' duration must be assumed before it can reach actuality. Matters can't be changed by just hooraying for and then printing groovy new ideas. It all takes time. One may rail against "bureaucratic sluggishness" but still benefit from the stately procedures that are intended to protect the national government from ill-considered haste.

Anyone involved in the granting world (applicants, reviewers, and evaluators) must learn first of all to think long, very long, much longer than one would ever think necessary. Three years from first thinking of the idea to its actual occurrence with everything in place in the real world is about the minimum.

⌒⌒

Probably no issue has so continually absorbed the Folk Arts Program as how best to select, recruit, instruct, employ, energize, recompense, and calm advisory panelists. Many people believe that this is the area where the Fearsome Federal Bureaucrat has secretly acquired control. This was not my experience. Indeed, I found myself distributing to new panelists a *New Yorker* cartoon in which desperate, thirsty castaways are crawling through sand dunes toward a meeting table behind which sits a group of stern, formally dressed, behatted ladies and gentlemen. The caption (from the castaways): "Thank God! A panel of experts!"

The Folk Arts staff was forever longing for just that: a panel of experts to provide us some reassurance, some bit of professional comfort. After all, we were open to emotionally rooted demands from every ethnic, occupational, and religious group in the entire nation. We tried to respond sensitively and intelligently—we always tried, but often we failed. And my goodness, did we need advice!

Long before I joined the NEA staff I had served on several Music Program panels assembled by the spirited and spiritual Walter Anderson, longtime director of the NEA's formidable Music Program and a man who had the gift of always being positive—in exactly the right place, at the right time, with the exactly right point of view. Because of his kindly urging, I had found myself taking a many a red-eye into Washington during the 1970s to participate in his panels.

And on such mornings I would often wake up and wonder which coast I was on—a tricky state of mind from which to judge a host of applications to the Jazz/Folk/Ethnic Music panel (as if they weren't complex enough all by themselves). But serving on that strangely titled panel was an important education for me, for I was forced to wind my way through the intertwining categorizations and gentle distinctions that each panelist held dear and that all panelists eventually had to agree to.

Later, when I myself attempted to formulate an appropriate "panel of experts" to help adjudicate the Folk Arts Program's grants, I looked back to my earlier experiences. The problem was still immense. Every panelist had to be able to think in terms of the needs of many cultures and many artistic disciplines; but each must also come from one or possibly more particular ethnic, regional, and/or professional backgrounds. The balancing out of their refined qualities in order to nominate a well-balanced and knowledgeable panel was, I often felt, the most complex problem I faced.

For *I* had to invite them—I myself (admittedly, after a great deal of consultation). But it was *my* job, and *I* invited them and warned them what to expect if they came, and *I* was responsible for their comfort and good spirits while they were in town. But who should these folks be? What kinds of skills and information should they represent?

Putting folk artists themselves on a Folk Arts panel always seemed the logical thing to do, but at that time it turned out to be extremely difficult. Many traditional artists proved acutely unhappy at being asked to judge other traditional artists, especially in unfamiliar cultures or disciplines. Some simply left the panel and went home. And then there were all those miles and miles of miscellaneous reading in the application books. Many artists, traditional and otherwise as well, announced that their time was more valuably spent doing their own work. Reading grant applications was just too specialized and difficult and took up too much of their creative time. And I have to say, I rather agreed with them.

Academics or other such professionals were easier to fit into the panel culture. Most of them made marvelous contributions, and they generally turned out to be the backbone of our panels. We also used business people and retirees from various cultural organizations. Even so, many well-qualified panelists simply could not afford to attend even an expense-paid three- or four-day meeting in Washington. No matter how patriotic they were, they still had to keep their day jobs and they couldn't get away for so long. Some eventually had to sacrifice a substantial piece of their vacation time in order to work for the Folk Arts Program.

But in spite of everything, our panels were simply splendid. We prepared mammoth grants books for panelists to read before they came (some reported their biceps had increased measurably since joining us). But the panelists always came prepared. They labored, they debated, they listened to performance recordings, they looked at slides and watched films. And they continually brought to the discussion a host of cheerful, outside-Washington points of view that kept us both lively and humble.

In connection with a routine application for recording funds, one panelist pointed out that it reminded him of the old popular song "If You've Got the Money, Honey, I've Got the Time," forever summing up for us the personality of the chronic professional application writer. Another panelist postulated the existence of a mythical "folklore police" that could be called upon to harry ill-considered projects. "This," he would majestically proclaim, "is without doubt a case for The Folklore Police."

And then there was one instance in which a panelist inquired whether we couldn't possibly award an applicant a grant if they would just guarantee *not* to do their proposed project. (I later found that that decision was outside the panel's prerogatives, but there it remains in the panel notes.)

In the early days we tried to (and actually did) achieve unanimity in panel decisions. As more and more requests poured in, we reluctantly decided that we could not afford the time necessary to attain 100 percent agreement; we would have to revert to majority rule. Debate was invariably brisk, substantive, passionate, and, I truly believe, fair. The field of folk arts was and is so small, and yet so broadly spread, that the issue of personal favoritism rarely came up even during the inevitable post-panel mourning, when everyone grieved over the things they wished had happened. (Chairman Livingston Biddle once commented that every time he signed off on any NEA grant, he realized that he had made twenty enemies along with only one friend.)

The aftermath of all this labor and passion was also problematic. Almost all applicants had taken a great deal of trouble, some of them for the first time ever, to get their applications in, with help from the Folk Arts staff all along the way. But inevitably most of the applications had to be eliminated—there simply was not enough money; and I must state that, for all the energy and time put in to them, they were all not equally competitive. But to be *rejected* was truly intolerable and brought us deep unhappiness. I began to try to explain the situation to unsuccessful applicants this way: "Suppose there was this wonderful potluck supper, and everybody brought their special dish, and the people running the event had decorated everything really beautifully with flowers and parsley, and the food was all arranged on the table looking and smelling so wonderful. And then the people came to eat it, but they simply couldn't eat it all. Different ones may have decided differently, taking a taste of every dish, but others decided to eat special things—chili and fried chicken and steamed clams and passion fruit salad. The point is that if everybody didn't choose your dish, it wasn't because they thought it wasn't any good—they just didn't have room for it."

Ultimately, I believe that the area in which the Folk Arts panels did their most important service was not so much in deciding who should and who should not get a grant, but in their ever responsible and sensitive observations about the conduct of work in this field. Nobody else was in a position to make such recommendations, and it was a hard and draining effort.

After an unusually petulant scrutiny of a particular application budget, during which its estimated prices for supplies and similar minutia had been cut down by critical panelists to the least possible amount, one of those panelists observed, "I believe we have now reached a truly significant figure. We are proposing to give these folks the *exact* amount of funds guaranteed to entice them to go ahead with this project, at the same time ensuring that they will not have *quite* enough money to be able to succeed with it." (We'd been agonizing over the parsley.)

What a lesson. Although I have decided to avoid mentioning most people's names as I go along, I cannot resist saying that this wise and memorable statement was made by Clydia Nahwooksy, a Cherokee friend, who told me once that when she returned home from Washington she often went to her grandfather for a cleansing ceremony.

I wish the Folk Arts staff could have been included. We had to stay on in Washington, getting all the recommended grants ready for review by the National Council on the Arts, along with the cleanup that inevitably follows a three- or four-day meeting, before we began getting ready for the next. (Most of the time we had four panel sessions per year—a killing schedule.) In between meetings I tried to sandwich in the time to organize my own perceptions of just what had happened at the last one.

I started out looking at the grants we had just recommended, dividing them into a series of often overlapping categories: states where the work would be done; amount of money to be awarded; type of activity (exhibition, festival, concert series, or tour); national, ethnic, or religious groups to be affected by the project; documentation methods (recordings, photography, or film). As I worked, ongoing problems became visible: the infrequency of projects in Asian arts, particularly performance; the infrequency of projects concerned with radio production; the infrequency of craft- or dance-focused projects, in comparison with those concerned entirely with music.

But there was always something more that seemed wrong to me about my attempts to work out the involvement of ethnicities. I felt generally uncomfortable about this whole area, and I couldn't figure out what was wrong. I had included in my various analyses all the Italian regional styles that identified themselves here; I had different categories for Ireland, Scotland, and Wales; most of the British material was accommodated under Appalachia. And then one day it came to me: I remembered a student who, in his required brief autobiography where I asked him how he identified himself, wrote bitterly, "I have no culture. Everybody else is a this or a that, but I am nobody at all." Well, of course he did have a culture, and I managed to help him realize it during the following semester, but I never forgot his shattering anger. As I tried to jiggle our figures to convince myself that we had indeed included everybody, I gradually realized that there was indeed an enormous number of people who simply weren't there at all in spite of all my inclusionary efforts.

Basically, we had left out the entirety of mid-America. Not in terms of geographic representation—we had plenty of good grants going to mid-western states—but in terms of the strong prevailing midwestern culture pattern. I wasn't the only one to suffer this intellectual blackout. I gradually came to realize that the Folk Arts Program represented only a tiny part of a great national dilemma.

So I went on back to work.

FOURTEEN

Working with States and Artists

The guidelines were in place and all was working well—but just not quite well enough. There were too many unexplored opportunities, too many lacunae in my beautiful map, too few announcements the Folk Arts Program could make with pride. Somehow we were not connecting very well outside our own group. We had discovered that we could not legally conjoin with other federal agencies, such as the Library of Congress or the Smithsonian, in joint fiscal sponsorship of the same project—an early effort of mine— and most public foundations seemed already to be quite satisfied with their limited contributions to our little-known field.

The NEA's requirement that grant applicants needed to put up half the costs of their proposed project, like most general rules, turned out to have its down as well as its up side. Certainly it served to discourage excessively costly, off-the-cuff, or simply inappropriate requests. However, appallingly few folk arts organizations or community groups were coming to us anyway, because they didn't have the required nonprofit status (it had just never occurred to them that they could possibly become profit making). All we really had to offer anybody was money, and the people we wanted to hear from either didn't have any to put up for a match or thought they didn't.

We began to cast about for other places where some reasonable-sized pots of money available for modest grant requests might be found. During our research we discovered that by federal law the NEA, in addition to its grants to arts institutions, had to send a sizable allocation of federal money to each state in the Union, depending on its size and population. I began to wonder if we could persuade some of the wealthier state arts agencies that they might further increase their NEA funding by obtaining *additional* contributions from an Endowment program. Indeed, the Folk Arts Program itself could possibly provide them with monies that they themselves would have to match out of their own funds; this would allow them to create small state-based folk arts programs and enable them to hire extra personnel to do the work. The state arts agency movement was already growing and feisty; this might be also a good way to join forces with such agencies.

There already were a few state folklorist positions out there, mostly unfilled, but we had a different idea in mind. We wanted to set up statewide positions, and we decided to call them "coordinators" because nobody could tell what a "coordinator" would do, thus maximizing the possibilities for action. My brother and I had argued about the concept from the beginning. Alan had said that he thought the old western pictures had the big story right: the good guy (a folklorist, of course) rides into town, gets things changed around and gets everything going well, and then, most important, he *rides out again*, allowing things to continue (maybe) or sink back (maybe) or strike off in a new direction (maybe). And maybe Alan was right, but so was I (maybe).

I started a general inquiry as to whether state arts agencies would be interested in our idea, and soon we began to get some nibbles, some discouraging and others merely inquisitive. One director called me to report enthusiastically that he had already located a great folk arts candidate for his agency: "You'd love her, Bess, she lives in a tree!" Finally, we put our ideas into writing, stating plainly that any position receiving Folk Arts Program funding had to require a person who had received an academic degree (preferably in folklore or ethnomusicology) as well as having had practical experience in arts presentation, whether through radio, recordings, press releases, documentary films, or festivals. Any such person must be employed full time to do work in this field and be paid in accordance with similar agency professionals.

We pointed out to the state arts agencies that paying attention to their area's folk and traditional arts was advantageous to them in several ways. For one thing, a local program could include such arts as quilting and carving that were familiar and friendly-sounding to many of their residents. Practitioners and enthusiasts of such arts were themselves scattered all over the scenery, and their recognition would give state programs a presence in communities that couldn't hope to house or support a ballet or opera company. Finally, the whole field of the traditional arts was an area for which political support was a new and generally appealing idea; getting into it would make them groundbreakers.

The idea proved not only appealing but well timed, and it eventually proved to be the linchpin in our attempts to develop sponsors for folk activities around the country. There were two reasons for its success: the arts world in general was in a growthsome period, the state arts agencies being especially healthy; and, overall, the entire nation was interested in investigating its cultural heritage. By the time I left the NEA, more than fifty states and territories had, at one time or another, set up programs—some failing, some being reinstated, and others blooming. One well-thought-of state agency director said that he believed that in the future any state that did *not* house a folk arts coordinator would come to be thought of as hopelessly out of date.

After enjoying the professionalism that our coordinators were displaying, some agency staffs were further strengthened. Almost everyone involved seemed reasonably happy and things were going along swimmingly, until the apparently irresistible trend toward functional reorganization (à la the National Endowment for the Humanities) set in. Gradually, painfully, the state programs began to disappear. But overall, the idea of a state folk arts coordinator refused to die and kept reappearing in historical societies, universities, regional arts coalitions, off and on in a whole variety of disguises.

Most agencies had indeed benefited by having professionally qualified people added to their staffs, and in general they had chosen well. I cannot possibly list all the great state folk arts coordinators—indeed, there soon became so many I could not possibly have gotten to know them all. (There were, of course, a few people hired who turned out to be day-to-dayers, but most rose to this exciting new possibility and let themselves go.)

Driving through North Dakota, a newly hired coordinator was struck by the number of towering wrought-iron structures he saw abandoned and often half-buried by the roadways. On inquiry, they proved to be remnants of long-forgotten grave markers. His photographic documentation was exhibited in the state museum, where it aroused such general interest that the governor instituted a search to find any remaining welders trained in the complex German-born skill and commissioned a new example for the capitol grounds. And many Dakotans who saw the show realized that the markers had been there all along; they were simply so familiar, nobody saw them any more.

Visiting the many small islands that make up the state of Hawaii was expensive and time consuming for any state employee, so the state's visually talented folk arts coordinator produced a series of exquisite picture postcards containing brief information about her program with glowing photographs of flower leis, leather work, and palmetto weaving by exceptionally talented Hawaiian craftsworkers. She continually used these to write her thank you notes, thereby transmitting news to people she had met during her visits, keeping in continual personal touch with her far-flung constituency.

Each state varied from the next in geography, politics, cultural distributions, population densities, and a myriad of other significant factors, forcing a special kind of creativity on the state folk arts workers. Opposite situations produced opposite responses. North Carolina, a long, thin state that reaches from the Atlantic Ocean to the heart of the Appalachians, was celebrated in a major first-time state folk festival organized by the talented coordinator, who set up the whole thing on a long, thin piece of land where traditional artists of each special section of the state could celebrate their arts together in their own special place on the "map," producing a vivid demonstration of the cultural excitement a trip through North Carolina has to offer. Every single member of the legislature attended that festival in order to have his picture taken with the grouped-together folk artists of his own domain. Again, this was a picture already familiar to old-time Carolinians; they already knew it but just hadn't thought about it that way.

Louisiana, by contrast, was already full of small, undeveloped rural communities, each having already started its own sweet-corn shucking or crawdad hunt or "mammoth" gumbo festival. There the state coordinator decided that his work might be better employed by visiting the plethora of established local events, providing information on the potential availability of overlooked local traditions, improved sound engineering, and available loan equipment, thereby helping renew the spirits of these ongoing occasions. In other states, the coordinators brought examples of the finest local crafts to the governor and showed that they could be used at little cost as official presents to distinguished visitors. The list could go on and on.

A further great service of the state coordinator idea was to relieve us of the responsibility for ailing or impossible federal projects. For example, we had from the beginning included in our federal guidelines a section of grants to persons who were not beginners, but who could benefit from study with senior traditional artists. We called such projects "apprenticeships" and we simply loved the whole idea, but we never could make it work on a federal level. We received remarkably few applications for such grants; the whole idea that the federal government would pay for somebody's summerlong study with an Appalachian fiddler or a Pueblo potter just never got off the page.

However, a number of state arts agencies took it on and it simply took off. Some thirty-six states supported some kind of apprenticing eventually, and it proved one of their most popular programs. Again, there were great differences between programs. In Alaska, the whole payment relationship had to be skewed around a trifle because the native peoples were offended by the suggestion that elders should be paid to teach young learners—things were already going along well, they said. Puerto Rico, on the other hand, found that it was more necessary to get funds directly to young learners than to elders; likely young learners often had to go to San Juan and work in hotels in order to contribute to their family income and couldn't afford "idle" time. But overall the concept was widely popular. Almost everyone easily understood the general idea and the reasons behind it and agreed that the old-timey or new-timey skills should be passed along and not forgotten.

As Barry Bergey (the Folk Arts Program folklorist who kept a special eye out for apprenticeship programs) and I wrote in an article for a National Association of State Arts Agencies publication: "As with forests and friendships, deeply rooted cultural apprenticeships tend to stand the test of time. This mysterious process succeeds in the long run where there is a timely confluence of aptitude and attitude, grounded in a sympathetic cultural terrain. Like so many good ideas, the concept of apprenticeships came to us quite unannounced from the past, a lesson of many masters from many places. And like good apprentices, the Folk Arts Program honors this time-tested concept through imitation."

Overall, the state programs brought a new vigor into our work; they spread the action out and developed a number of projects we never otherwise could have heard from. Local traditional groups took on new life, regional associations began to form, fascinating people kept stopping by or phoning up. Like the rest of the arts world, we were in a buzz.

So far I have been speaking as though the traditional arts that interested the Folk Arts Program were generally easy to locate, in good shape, and the foregrounded pride of their communities. Actually, none of these conditions were frequent. Most traditional arts that emerged during my NEA period turned up vaguely recalled, politicized, malleable, anxious, and/or generally ignored.

In 1988 or 89, I was standing near a market center near the outskirts of the American Samoan capital Pago Pago when a young mother came by me juggling a vigorous lap baby and three sizable coconuts. Her situation was clearly unmanageable, but she walked to the side of the dirt road, laid the baby down in the grass, pulled a couple of fronds off a roadside palmetto, sat herself down, and in five or ten minutes wove a basket. It wasn't a great basket, I suppose, nor was it an aesthetically compelling basket, but it held three coconuts and that's what she needed a basket to do right then. It had a handle that fit over her arm and a nice solid bottom, and the lady put the coconuts in it, slung her baby over her shoulder, and took off up the hill.

I was dazzled—I had never seen anybody do such a thing before—and I mentioned it later to a Samoan friend who provided an addendum. This was what everyone used to do when they had a lot to carry, he remarked. When they got back up to their mountain homes they would use these temporary palmetto baskets until they began to come apart, and then they would throw them into one of the many little streams that ran down from the central Samoan mountains to the sea. Nobody thought anything about it.

He added that nowadays lots of people have money to buy imported plastic sacks that work really well and look really stylish up to the point where they, too, wear out and are then thrown into the little streams. But plastic sacks in little streams don't rot; they sit there forever and clog up the waterway, or if they manage to make it to the ocean they wash back and forth endlessly on the beaches. Unlike palmetto baskets, plastic sacks never deteriorate. I myself, every morning of my Samoan stay, pulled twenty or so plastic bags out of the sea where I swam in front of my comfortable hotel. I didn't really know what to do with them and finally piled them up in a corner of the beach, where they may well be to this day. It takes a *long* time for a plastic sack to disintegrate.

Basketry, in general, had long been a thorny though always lovable issue for the Folk Arts Program. Influenced by popular thought, NEA staffers tended to refer all basketry projects to us because they felt baskets were probably folk art (since they didn't seem to be anything else). But at that time many people also tended to use the term "basket making" as a shorthand expression for any pitifully easy, useless college course. The word had a terrible reputation. Could—should—the Folk Arts Program, so small, new, and vulnerable, get involved with Samoan "basket making"? Aside from the fact that nobody had asked us to poke into that particular problem anyway, I wondered was it anybody's business but the Samoans'? And if not theirs or ours, then whose? Nobody, including any Samoans, had ever discussed this particular situation with the Folk Arts Program.

But here is what I saw: the basket that the young mother made was a survival of an elegant solution to a practical problem. Over the ages other solutions had also become possible, but this one fitted its situation perfectly, and its exercise, over time, seems to have resulted in a general feeling of confidence within the local population that this particular choice could, indeed, take care of this particular difficulty. And so, although nobody thought much about it, almost all Samoans routinely learned how to make a basket because probably one day they would need one. And, at least when I was visiting there, there seemed to be confidence within the local population that this was the way the basket situation was, for now and for the reasonable future.

In the fullness of time, if a great many baskets are needed or desired, there may be an outburst of new designs to keep ennui at bay or to keep the interest of an especially fine basket maker. Of course, it may turn out that the local population will elect the mercantile (plastic bag) solution; then, because of the eventual befouling of their waters, this may in time require the Samoans to work out some method of destroying or recycling those indestructible plastic bags. (I have no doubt future folklorists will enjoy tracking their creative solutions.)

I myself, as the years went by, became more and more convinced that basket making is a culturally vital activity, often crucial to the psychic well-being of a particular group. There are enormous numbers of people who typically make baskets—not only American Indian tribes (all of whom have their own variations on the craft), but the descendants of European settlers from Appalachia through the Midwest, African Americans on the southern U.S. coast, and every people throughout the entire Pacific area from Alaska through Micronesia, Melanesia, and Polynesia. Different peoples have different values—often practical, but artistic and spiritual as well—attached to basketry. I began to feel it was a tremendously undervalued topic. Basket Making 101, indeed! We had to get the topic into a larger context.

Are traditional crafts only a kind of prolonged primitive technology? This was a question we had to deal with early in the history of the Folk Arts Program (and we kept on and on dealing with it, by the way).

One of our earliest grant applications came from a young cultural center on the South Carolina coast. On our huge wall map, it sat in the middle of an eastern seaboard region that seemed isolated, complex, and full of possibilities, and it hosted an extraordinarily rich deposit of African American traditional culture. In terms of performing arts, citizens of that area enjoyed jazz marching bands as fresh as those in New Orleans, as well as the glorious sonorities of Daddy Grace trombone choirs, religious singing from old-fashioned shape note hymn books, and the powerful dynamic interweaving of gospel songs. There were quieter songs too: solo lullabies and love songs and the blues—the old-fashioned blues, a man and his guitar or his harmonica talking to himself or to his love.

And in material culture there was more pure gold: marvelously diverse, dazzlingly contrastive quilts, many in the distinctive "strip" patterns that recall the narrow, horizontal stripes of East African weaving. And as various scholars looked into the local basketry tradition, it became more and more clear: this was historically rice country, and rice and basketry always go together. Consider, for a moment, how one might handle a pour of rice grains *without* having a metal bucket or a clay pot or—lighter, more accessible, and cheaper—a tightly woven basket.

A respected researcher who went door-to-door throughout Charleston County, South Carolina, reported that every single person in that county older than a lap baby could make a basket. Not all of them did, of course, and many didn't consider themselves especially good at it, but everybody *could* make a basket. If Rumpelstiltskin had demanded the overnight production of a basket—or else horrible things would ensue—anybody in Charleston County could thumb a nose at him. Even leaving Rumpelstiltskin out of it, 100 percent of anything is a truly memorable statistic.

Further, it seems extremely unlikely that *any* serious proportion of the residents of the neighboring, mostly Anglo-American counties could make a basket. They might be able to shine (or at least glow) in knot tying, embroidery, or whittling, and there are grapevine and split-oak baskets produced nearby by both Native American and Anglo-American weavers. But making tight, smooth sweetgrass baskets surpasses those efforts by far and is still a deep and essential function particular to the African American communities along the southeastern American coast.

The Folk Arts Program was privileged to observe the development of South Carolina coastal basket making over thirty-odd years, occasionally being asked for help, but mostly not. This did not slake our interest; we became gradually used to the fact that many groups everywhere only wanted to ooze along slowly, anyway, and did not thank us for attempting to pick up the pace. It was the accidents of history that brought many such situations into our remote but passionate federal view.

For a long time, the South Carolina basket makers had sold their wares out of roadside stands on the various highways into Charleston. But during the 1970s and 80s a number of long-term problems began to intensify. High-speed highway traffic was making roadside selling both dangerous and noxious. Also critical was the increasing physical scarcity of sweetgrass, the essential stalks around which other traditional fibers are wound in the act of making a Sea Island basket.

Sweetgrass is a somewhat temperamental wild crop that thrives primarily in the littoral—the land between the sea and the sand dunes. South Carolina basket makers (mostly women) have for many years encouraged foraging expeditions (mostly by men) up and down the Atlantic coast as far as central Florida, hoping to locate new available stands of sweetgrass. Although African American harvesting methods appear to do the least possible damage to the beach itself as well as to the remaining plant roots, the demand for baskets has been rising so quickly as to keep stocks of raw materials at a dangerously low level. More critically, the ever increasing fencing-off of large sections of the Atlantic shoreline by hotel and condominium investor/builders—often employing chain-link fences, attack dogs, and armed guards around their perimeters—has been preventing exploration, as well as the harvesting of known stands. It was, and still is, a dismaying situation.

At this point, the step-by-step historical progression gets less clear (or perhaps less important). One of the things the Folk Arts Program has learned over the years is that cultural issues often seem to evolve in response to a kind of prolonged, many-sourced cultural tickling. Things rarely progress in an orderly A to B to C fashion.

In the case of the Sea Island basket tradition, the local cultural center hired (with a small amount of federal money) a young anthropologist to look into the cultural history of the Sea Island craft traditions. He found interesting basketry correlatives in West Africa and he wound up producing a three-page fold-over leaflet illustrating the similarities between African and African American rice basketry. It was printed up by the cultural center (now, sadly, out of business).

But the leaflet isn't out of business. Some years ago I visited Charleston and its open-air market. When I bought a lovely Sea Island basket, the weaver stuffed a piece of paper inside before she gave it to me. "Oh, what's that?" I asked. "What's that" turned out to be a photocopy of that original, at least ten-year-old, anthropological leaflet. I asked the basket maker where she had gotten it, and she replied, "Well, every morning we all go over to the public library over there and we xerox as many copies as we think we'll need. And that's the way *that* is."

The South Carolina basket sellers (all women) had grown up in the tradition of West African market saleswomanship and had observed that buyers seemed to like the leaflets. And then some of them knew that the Smithsonian Institution similarly enhanced the craft objects it sold by affixing informational labels or tags. So they decided it seemed like a good thing to do.

The anthropologist who did the research, wrote the copy, and selected the illustrations for that brief but enormously influential leaflet may by now have reached an audience of half a million or even a million people—there is absolutely no way to tell. I am sure he had no idea how far it would travel. Such a story is enough to make you polish like a jewel every single little light that you might help let shine. These days, they can shine so far.

But to return to the basket makers: at one point the State of South Carolina attempted, via traffic ordinances, to eliminate the highway basketry stands (possibly as being undignified). The mayor of Charleston countered with his own brilliant concept of the "cultural easement"—in this case, a local ordinance that allows only basketry, or similar cultural artifacts, to be displayed and sold along highways leading into the city.

But these peaceable artists seem destined to remain in the heart of drama. The southeastern coast of the United States can be stormy, and it often takes the brunt of advancing hurricanes. A particularly ferocious one recently destroyed the basket makers' stands and their purchasable stock; and vast stands of sweetgrass from which the baskets could be replaced simply disappeared as well, washed out to sea. But the basket makers continue to hang in there. They have formed a basket makers' organization, and they have studied the governmental system and learned how to apply for emergency help when needed. The Sweetgrass Basket Makers Association has become a respected voice in the local political and arts scene.

In 1984 a senior basket maker, Mary Jane Manigault, received a National Heritage Award from the Folk Arts Program of the National Endowment for the Arts. Lincoln Caplan, writing in the "Talk of the Town" column in the *New Yorker* magazine on October 1 that year, described an episode in part of the celebration as follows:

> In the Mike Mansfield Room, Emily Zuttermeister, whose maiden name was Kau'i-o-Makaweli-na-lani-o-Ka-Mano-o-Ka-lani-po, chanted a sacred Hawaiian chant, an invocation to the gods of nature for peace and blessings on the beautiful earth; Clifton Chenier strapped on his accordion to play some loud, rollicking Creole music known as *zydeco*. A frail, graceful woman named Elizabeth Cotten, who is ninety-one, sang "Freight Train," which she wrote when she was twelve. All but one of seventeen winners of the 1984 National Heritage Fellowships, each given by the National Endowment for the Arts to "a Master Traditional Artist who has contributed to the shaping of our artistic traditions and to preserving the cultural diversity of the United States, . . ." [were there]. No one seemed more at home in that atmosphere than Howard (Sandman) Sims.
>
> Mr. Sims, who is from 123rd Street and Seventh Avenue, in Harlem, wore a Nike cap, a crisp tan warm-up suit, and Pony sneakers, and had a bright-green amulet on a chain around his neck. He is known as the Sandman . . . after a dance that he executes by pouring a pocketful of sand on a poster-size board and scratching out the chug of a train in motion. . . . "I was *born* dancing," he said in a patient tone. "I'm *still* dancing. I can't *quit* dancing. I dance a *whole lot*. . . . Here's what I do. I teach you, you get it down, and you show someone else. That's it."
>
> The Sandman walked us over to look at some coiled baskets made from sweetgrass. "There's nothing in the world that's sweeter than these," he informed us. "There ain't a weave out of line." He turned to a short, white-haired woman nearby, introduced her as Mary Jane Manigault, from Mount Pleasant, South Caroline, who had won her award for a lifetime of weaving baskets, and spoke as if he were quoting from an official Sandman proclamation: "You can tell how she's thinking! Smooth! Beautiful! And she's teaching the youngsters how to do it!"
>
> The weaver laughed at the dancer and slapped him five. "The Lord does his thing through all of us," he declared. "Yeah," she answered. "We've got to pass it on," he continued, directing a series of brush steps toward a girl sitting close by. "I hear you," said Mary Jane Manigault, fingering a basket. "Pattern. Color. Everything," the Sandman summed up. "That's what they've got. Pass it on."

FIFTEEN

The National Heritage Fellowships

It was during my very first conversation with Nancy Hanks, then NEA chair, that she brought up the Living National Treasures of Japan. She felt strongly that the Arts Endowment ought to try such an idea in this country, and she asked me to consider the Folk Arts Program as a possible home site. At the time I felt doubtful, but I did try to look into just how the system had worked in Japan. At first I could find only a little printed in English, but what I was able to learn impressed me very much.

The entire idea seems to have grown from a longstanding and highly serious effort by the Japanese people to protect their cultural heritage. They had recognized the problem a very long time ago, and in 1950 numerous centuries-old local regulations of greatly varying types were consolidated into a remarkable piece of legislation that defined "Important Intangible Cultural Properties" as "intangible cultural products materialized through such human behaviors as drama, music, dance, and applied arts, which have a high historical value." At first only those Intangible Cultural Properties that were in possible danger of loss were placed under protection of the new law. Later the rule was relaxed and a registration system was set in place to include those of especially high artistic value, as well as those having "conspicuous local characteristics." As of 1983, fifty-nine kinds of crafts, seventy artists from other art forms, and eleven groups had been recognized and formally registered by the Japanese government as Holders of Important Intangible Cultural Properties.

Honorees receive a Living National Treasure Award, a recognition that is not to be taken lightly. An annual stipend goes with it, as do ongoing responsibilities to represent, further, and advance the highest standards of the particular art through demonstrations, teaching, and continued practice. Those honored may be invited to testify on matters concerning the arts, to host visiting delegations, to judge contests, to settle controversies—in all, to concern themselves in every way with the needs of the art form and its practitioners. In the meantime, the government both purchases their works and keeps records, through film and other types of documentation, of the techniques and methods used to produce them. It also supports annual exhibitions of their work, maintains a registry of private and public owners of important traditional art pieces, and provides a grants program for those who wish to learn, practice, or study the art form.

This complex, multifaceted, and thoughtful system arose in Japan in the mid-nineteenth century, when a three-hundred-year period of national isolation came to an end and the nation's doors were at last opened. This stimulated a headlong plunge into European-influenced modernization, which in turn raised fears that the older, peculiarly Japanese art forms that had become so exquisitely refined during isolation might be shoved aside, allowed (or encouraged) to degenerate, or be forgotten. Clearly this was a matter of national concern, for the response of the Japanese people to these fears was to devise a truly remarkable structure of cultural statesmanship. The Important Intangible Cultural Properties program has had powerful effects in its own country and has set high standards for the rest of the world.

However, when I tried to imagine such a system functioning in the United States, I came up against two major difficulties. The first was the simple issue of time depth: it takes time for a culture to make significant changes. The current system in Japan has been in place for over fifty years, and before that almost a century of worried attempts, improvised pieces of local legislation, institutional rulings, and manifestoes by no longer extant councils and artists' organizations had delved into the problem from every possible point of view. The tradition of considering indigenous Japanese art forms to be of genuinely national importance had been in place for at least a century and a half, not even mentioning the three centuries of isolation before.

The second difficulty was one of mind-set. I cannot explore here the history of official and unofficial attitudes toward either indigenous or imported art in the United States, but it is very clear that we haven't had much practice in thinking about a national approach to either kind. The general lack of concern for (or even interest in) the arts traditional to small groups made the introduction of a brand-new system of recognizing those art forms extremely chancy and full of peril.

During the last of the period of Japanese isolationism, the United States was itself taking an opposite course: encouraging immigration and welcoming the arrival of ever larger populations, at least from some sections of the world, so as to increase the available work force. Some interested Americans have worried that such large numbers of newly arrived immigrant peoples, complete with their own cultural pasts and presents, might dilute or even radically alter the national character. However, the comforting hypothesis that there existed a national "melting pot"—an enormous all-encompassing crucible into which all contending artistic and cultural traditions would contentedly dissolve to emerge as true-blue Americans (while retaining their Old World color and charm)—appeased the worst jingoists. The slow but steady abandonment of local and ethnic traditions that took place in the early twentieth century could then be cited as proof of the efficacy of "the American way." We did indeed have a system in place, but it was one that was not especially interested in those art forms "with conspicuous local characteristics," as the Japanese put it—in other words, the folk arts.

In spite of the formidable problems just mentioned, the Important Intangible Cultural Properties concept continued to exert a fundamental appeal. Most people just loved the whole idea and it refused to die, so in the late 1970s, Folk Arts Program advisory panels began to take up the topic of a system to provide individual awards and honorifics for American folk artists.

As I had rather expected, all the panels consulted for several years were intrigued by the general concept of some kind of living national treasures program, but they had a number of new and interesting objections to raise. Folk arts, they pointed out, are above all the cultural possessions of groups rather than of individuals, whether those groups affiliate themselves by virtue of sharing a religion, occupation, ethnicity, geographical area, language, or any other common factor. In the United States, with its long history of religious freedom, open immigration, and industrial expansionism, there are enormous numbers of observable folk groups, all of which have, to a greater or lesser extent, developed active artistic traditions. How could one even begin to ascertain the number of groups that should be considered in such a program? How could one begin to locate them?

Then, since the traditional art forms have generally been developed by vast numbers of people over time within each group, who was going to say which individual practitioner should be the particular one honored? And if we could achieve consensus as to which tradition to honor and which artist was preeminent in it, would not this public recognition have a dampening effect on the artists *not* selected and, thereby, on the art form itself? Would it not create jealousies or stimulate unhealthy competition? Overall, might the attempt to further an art form by this means have a discouraging or distorting effect—exactly the opposite of what was intended?

Oh, dear. We debated it this way and we debated it that. We considered the effect of such an award on an individual carver in a remote New Mexico Hispanic village, as well as on Serbian American urban steelworker/musicians in a neighborhood band. We came to no conclusion and put the idea to rest, only to have it rise up again the next year before a new panel and before another panel in another year after that. I believe I am accurate in stating that in all these many discussions nobody ever exactly wanted to do it, but everybody thought it ought to be tried.

At long last in 1980 a recommendation was made that the National Endowment for the Arts should set up a program to recognize each year an unspecified number of individual traditional artists, who would be selected from nominees proposed by the general public. Each artist would receive a certificate of honor and a check for five thousand dollars (a sum that was agreed upon as being impressive but not so great as to encourage any recipient to change a lifetime's living pattern). This proposal went before the National Council on the Arts, and there, to our considerable surprise, a whole new series of objections arose.

The legislation that originally set up the National Endowment for the Arts had been especially cunningly crafted to forestall any conceivable possibility that partisan politics might affect the development of the nation's cultural future. The Arts Endowment was not to select official artists or fund official structures; it was not to do anything, however insignificant, that could conceivably smack of governmentally sponsored or "approved" art. The agency was designed to help all kinds of art grow, develop, and flourish, and to ensure that art would succeed or fail not according to official federal standards, but ultimately according to the response of its multiple audiences. And the National Heritage Program (as we had come to call it) came uncomfortably close, in many council members' opinions, to a kind of governmental sanction, a federal seal of approval. In fact, it came close to being an "award"—a privilege that is very properly allowed to only a very few parts of the federal government. In point of fact, the agency was simply not legally authorized to give any kind of honorary recognition awards. And that was that.

I have to say that the entire Folk Arts Program was stunned. It had taken a long time to get this far, and we argued with vigor for our point of view, but gradually we began to find ourselves reluctantly agreeing with the council's reservations. Actually, their concerns formed an interesting mirror for the panels' concerns; in a way, each represented a side of the same problem. We would have to work on the original plan itself, and we began to shift our recommendation slightly.

The first change sounds like a bureaucratic double-shuffle but, like the best administrative ploys, it had a far greater significance. We decided the five-thousand-dollar checks should be referred to not as "awards" but as "fellowships," which could be interpreted as simple contributions toward the artistic future of the particular recipient. This not only made the grants legally approvable, but moved the program back toward the idea of the "living treasures," which we had begun to lose sight of. We also decided to recognize each year a relatively large number of artists—perhaps ten or twelve rather than only one or two; the program would then be just another part of our ongoing workaday endeavors to demonstrate the wide-ranging variability of the traditional arts in our nation.

After we had finally gotten the whole thing moving, it began to appear that the fellowships had become a great instrument for informing the American people about their own cultural history. Nothing else we ever did aroused so much public interest or scored as highly with everyone who heard about it. I shouldn't have been surprised. The recipients happily accepted the awards, and everyone felt that their own special favorite would probably get one some time or other. The entire "Happy Birthday" syndrome had swung merrily into effect, and we had hit the cultural jackpot.

There was certainly no dearth of suitable artists: one year, indeed, the nominating panel recommended seventeen, a number that turned out to be self-defeating, since no one could remember all the artists selected. The substitution of "fellowship" for "award" had, however, resulted in the fact that no deceased artist could be recognized, and that produced some heartbreak. But basically, year after year, ten or twelve amazingly exciting, vibrant, and joyful artists, from every state of the union, practicing every possible kind of traditional skill, have received recognition from their federal government, and the entire operation shows no sign of slacking off.

The downsides that have emerged have not proved lethal, the most serious perhaps being not internal, but external. The Folk Arts Program had to add the evaluation of individuals to the evaluation of projects, and this created a vast amount of new work for everybody—staff and panelists—as well as a subtle but appreciable change in overall perspective. It was the closest we had ever come to participating in mass culture, and the association showed. A new perspective had to be added to our accustomed considerations of community nature and needs: the evaluation of individual talents. It made everyone—staff and panelists—a tiny bit competitive, and the aromas of private interests or the occasional quid pro quo understanding began to rise up, mercifully on rare occasions. My somewhat myopic focus on the external had left me quite unprepared for any of this.

But the selected artists were happy as clams, and everybody else plowed on joyfully too. We realized that this would be the first time many of the awardees would ever be in Washington, so we arranged for their elegant certificates to be presented on Capitol Hill, the Senate side alternating with the House. Although they took place in august historical rooms full of draperies and paintings, the presentations themselves were always lively occasions. Generally, the commendations and awards were made by NEA chairs, but on three occasions the First Lady (then Hillary Clinton) did the honors herself. The artists were given several opportunities to show their skills informally, people from all over the capital were attracted (including congress members and senators congratulating their local artists), and we often had a hard time getting everyone out of there so that other national business could go forward.

That same evening, we hosted a private formal dinner party for the awardees and their relatives, during which I asked all the recipients to speak about their art and their feelings about the events. At the 1990 banquet, the Piedmont blues singer John Cephas, who had received his fellowship the year before and had joined us as a local host, spoke eloquently and earnestly to the current "class," saying roughly, "Some of you folks are probably just thinking this is about the great bunch of money you're going to get or the fun you're having in Washington. But these awards are a whole lot bigger than that. They're going to change your lives. You're going to think about yourself and what you do differently, and other people are going to think about you differently too. Because now, you and what you do *mean* something." Other awardees thanked us effusively, still others talked about the difficulties of their art form and how little it was rewarded, others about their childhoods. It was a family evening and we all went home happy.

The next and final night was for the general public, especially the people of Washington. We held the event in the big downtown concert hall at Washington University, and it always thrilled me to look out and see the citywide range of residents who had come to see their own kind of folks on the big stage. They made great audiences: they roared and applauded, and always some of them told me that it was the best show in town. One charming lady earnestly recommended to a delighted Charles Kuralt (that night's emcee) that he ought to try going on television, he was so good.

The concert itself was always a rewarding experience. Sometimes we were able to project the words being sung on a rear screen over the stage, and the emotional impact of the serious and eloquent lyrics of ancient Hawaiian hulas and contemporary Chicano corridos simply soared. Unforeseeable dramas sometimes occurred before our eyes: one evening the aging banjo genius Earl Scruggs, who believed he could no longer play, was gently persuaded onto the stage by his longtime friend and neighbor John Hartford and gradually joined the bluegrass band assembled in his honor. It turned out he could still play pretty well, even in his own eyes.

After the final bows, the honorees, all the staff, and particular friends repaired to a basement room under the auditorium for some modest refreshments and heartfelt good-byes. All of us would be going home the next day, and the intense, though often quite improbable, friendships that had simply appeared during the exciting few days of celebration (like the one that bloomed between a tiny Hmong *gaeng* musician and a lanky black urban street poet who accompanied himself with breathtakingly complex body-slapping) just dissolved, I suppose, into memory.

For we never found out what happened afterward to any of the honorees, really. We got occasional glimpses. The Alabama legislature invited the great old black Sacred Harp singer Dewey Williams to lead a hymn before them in the statehouse. A Slovenian polka band from Wisconsin returned home, pooled their accumulated prize money, and set up a local bank account from which they could draw funding for an annual award to the best young polka group, informing me that they figured they could continue doing this for at least eight years more. But the reaction that, in many ways, I hold closest to my heart was that of the Mississippi blues player who remarked, when he got back home, that for the first time in his life he had finally gotten what he was worth.

SIXTEEN

Memories

Time kept going on and things kept changing. (Why shouldn't they? They always do.) A lot of unintended consequences showed up, some positive, some not. Most things just went along being complex and difficult.

One afternoon, it was almost dark in my turret office in the Old Post Office Building where I was working late. A lady came in and said, "Don't stop. I just want to rest here a minute." She was chair of one of the South Pacific Micronesian arts councils, a woman in her middle years, and I knew her, although not very well. She sat down over in a corner and I went on working. Finally I stopped, intending to suggest that we go out for a bit of supper together. When I looked over at her, she began to talk.

"Bess, I just heard today that the very last tiny piece of our little island has been sold by its last single owner to a Japanese or something organization that wants to put a four-story building on it. So now the land is all gone, every single piece of it; somebody else owns it. That was all that was left; the rest already belonged to Europeans or Americans or other Asians, and now our whole island does. And we did this to ourselves. Nobody made us do it; we just kept on and on thinking about all that lovely money we could have. And now I will never again be able to place my foot on a single spot of ground that was handed down by my ancestors and kept by my people."

I couldn't think what to say. She had quietly started to cry, and I went over and sat down by her and put my arms around her, and the two of us grieved together while the traffic noises died away and the stars began to come out in the evening sky. After a while we went home, each one to her own temporary rented space. I have never been able to think of what I could have said to her. Maybe there just wasn't anything.

So many people came to that tiny office of mine, and oddly often they turned up at the end of the day, a time when the Folk Arts Program might have looked like a vaguely possible final resort. One late afternoon, a young woman from a northern Plains tribe came into my office along with an obviously distinguished elder gentleman. We ladies had completed our business, which consisted mostly of my telling her sadly that Folk Arts neither had the money nor the jurisdiction to provide the help her people so obviously needed, when after a long silence the old gentleman spoke for the first time. "Did you ever see a tipi city?" he said to me, his opaque eyes turned toward the darkening window. And there was a long pause. The usual office noises had quieted down; nobody else was around. I hadn't ever and I told him so.

"Oh, you ought to have seen a tipi city," he told me, his old face shining with recollection. "My father showed me one time. He woke me in the middle of the night when I was just a little boy, and we walked all through the night, and in the very first light of morning I saw a tipi city. A whole *city* of tipis, shining as far as the eye could see. It was so beautiful—all white and pale, spread out there in the moonlight.

"And you know the wonderful thing about a tipi city, you couldn't *ever* get lost in a tipi city! My father showed me. If there were six poles or eight poles showing at the top that meant one tribe or the other, and if there was a fox tail hanging from one pole that meant one clan, and if there was a turkey wing, that was another. Once you learned the rules there wasn't any way you could *ever* get lost in a tipi city." And his hopeful old face beamed across the office.

After a bit, in accordance with the rules of Texas country hospitality, I escorted the old gentleman and his companion out to our bank of elevators to see them down to the streets of Washington, where I knew no turkey wing or fox tail would ever show them where they were, where no building would ever look anything like a tipi, where so many would always be lost. And I found myself hoping once again that the disciplines I have so long supported would rouse themselves in their full vigor to help mediate and preserve the human symbols that have meant so much to human kind. We don't know everything about how to do it, but we do know enough to go on with.

The years kept on going by, punctuated with remarkable conversations of the kind I have just recounted, and as things went along I found myself personally being honored, over and over again, wherever I went. Although I always appreciated these occasions, they were invariably uncomfortable for me.

I have long tried to overcome it, but I am, and have always been, deeply shy. General conversation with large numbers of strangers is always awkward for me—I strongly prefer taking them on one or two at a time. And then I am never, inside myself, quite sure what I am being honored for. I have singly produced no books, no films, no songs; all my creative work has been collaborative. I have never considered myself a naturally talented or especially efficient administrator either.

On the positive side, I am extremely hard to defeat. I rarely use the word "defeat" itself and I think of setbacks as temporary obstacles to be reexamined and taken care of at a more propitious time. There is always a large category of what seem to me very good ideas in the back of my mind, waiting for a favorable moment to try them once again. I believe I learned this from my brother.

I do not care for fighting and try to reserve my anger for the most critical issues. I have picked my fights very carefully and worked out many ways of avoiding direct conflict—sometimes too many, I am now afraid. I cloak my weaknesses, such as my absolute need to be able to evaluate problems slowly, by not giving my opinion until the last possible moment, when I might know better what I am doing. Overall, I believe my tempo is irritatingly slow, though difficult to block entirely.

None of these qualities, though perhaps admirable, seems to me worth public celebration. I have several times asked my old and trusted staffers why all these extraordinary honors were coming to me, and they have impatiently said, "Don't be silly, Bess, of course you know what you've done." But except that I have perhaps functioned as a catalyst for what most of us already knew, I still can't put my finger on it. Perhaps this is why I have written this long account of my adventures.

Receiving the National Medal of Arts from President Bill Clinton within such a diverse and glittering group as Walter and Leonore Annenberg, Cab Calloway, Ray Charles, Stanley Kunitz, Robert Merrill, Arthur Miller, Robert Rauschenberg, Lloyd Richards, William Styron, Paul Taylor, and Billy

Wilder was, however, downright glorious and not to be quibbled over—a truly gala affair throughout.

The awardees assembled in the White House early one afternoon at a formal reception to which I was escorted by my brother Alan, who had in an earlier year received the same medal from President Reagan. President Clinton was aware of this and mentioned it with amusement when we were introduced: the first brother/sister act, he pointed out, in the history of the awards. When we were being rounded up for the procession to the ceremony on the White House lawn, I found myself getting nervous and went over and introduced myself to Ray Charles, the friendliest face I saw at the moment. He was most cordial, and he even lit up a bit when I told him I was kind of scared. He told me confidentially that he was too, so we held hands through the walk out into the bright afternoon and up the steps to the platform.

President Clinton called each of us across the stage to receive the award, speaking personally to and about each honoree with humor and dignity. At the grand dinner in the White House state dining room—all crystal and gold and sparkle—I sat in a place of honor next to Vice President Al Gore, who was cordial but aloof until someone else at the table threw out a practical political question, when he suddenly turned on and showed his tremendous energy and knowledge. My right-hand neighbor was Arthur Miller, who was greatly taken with his own right-hand lady, Anjelica Huston, who talked across Miller to me occasionally. I was really chopping in high cotton, I realized. The music (a great military brass unit), the gorgeous flowers, and the general atmosphere of brilliance and joy were all wonderful, and I can't remember when I enjoyed myself so much. This outstanding dinner party adjourned into another White House room where seats were set up for a concert by a group of young classical artists, whose performances were exquisite. President Clinton afterward commented gracefully that he was now going to be able to mark off "the future of music among young people" from the list of problems he keeps at his bedside. Finally, we all went off to dance to the marine corps dance band in the White House foyer, and my son, Nick, who was my escort for the evening, led me out onto the floor.

Afterward, though, I found my most frequently occurring memory of the great day was President Clinton's final remarks at the afternoon ceremony. I remembered them this way: "Well, folks, I'm sorry about this but we're all going to have to go. I have to go back in the White House and meet a congressional committee and Mrs. Clinton is entertaining some foreign dignitaries, and we just can't stay any longer. And I'm sure you have demanding things to do yourselves.

"But before we all go, I want us to take one more look at these people up on the platform here. Each one of them was born in a different place in a different part of America, in a different kind of house—small, large, out in the country, in cities. Some were rich, some were poor. They couldn't be more different. But they share one thing in common: at some point in their lives, they were caught by a great idea, a great question or problem around which they spent the rest of their lives. Each one of them. And when we leave here, I want every one of us personally to try to guarantee that every single child in our nation—not just these honorees up here—has the opportunity to be caught by his or her own great idea."

I was so moved by that speech that I never forgot it, and I told lots of people about it, including some classes I was teaching at the time. But later, when I wanted to write about this in my memoirs, I wrote the White House asking if a transcript of the president's remarks was still available, please could they send me a copy?

In due course "Remarks by the President in White House Presidential Arts Medal Ceremony" arrived, and after all the introductions and general remarks, I read his final words: "Remember, all the people we honor today were once in an ordinary community in an ordinary neighborhood living only with the imagination they had that brought them to this day and this honor. We have to find that imagination and fire it in the children all over America."

Overall, I think the president did a much better rhetorical job than I did. But occasionally I wonder what actually happened. I have always heard that the president was a gifted off-the-cuff speaker. Did he glance at some written, staff-generated remarks and then improvise the message as he wanted to send it at that particular moment? Or did he read the prepared text, and did I later improvise what I thought I had heard? Or did both things happen at the same time? We certainly did communicate: his energy and excitement and passion came just barreling across the White House lawn and I caught it all, right in my middle.

Well, probably it doesn't matter exactly how it happened, not really. But I see now that where I thought I had heard the president say "idea," he had (actually?) said "imagination"—and these are very different statements. One way of interpreting this disparity is that the president was speaking directly to the artists behind him, and I was thinking more of the children of the nation for whom imagination is only a small part of the artistic materials they will need to be able to utilize in the future. Again, in this area, analysis is probably more confusing than helpful.

Pete Seeger once firmly informed me that the story I had long told classes about his adventures learning to make and play the steel drum in Trinidad was completely untrue, that nothing of the kind I thought he had told me had ever happened. I was thunderstruck. (And I still don't see how I could possibly have made up every single bit of it.) So ever since when I tell this story, I have found myself saying something like, "Well, now. Pete says this is all completely wrong, but this is what I remember Pete telling me when he first got back from the Caribbean."

Long, long ago during an evening house party in Cambridge, before I even was an Almanac Singer, I sang a version of the old ballad about Montcalm and Wolfe. It was long and romantic and tense, and at the end I remarked that the events in the song were actually historically true. A very senior Harvard history professor in the audience remarked gently that there are two kinds of historical truth—what actually happened and what everybody *thought* happened—and he was also kind enough to add that the second kind seems sometimes more important than the first, because it so influenced what happened next.

I'm not at all sure of the importance of my own lengthy and complicated story, but I have tried hard to set down what I think happened. I have not checked it for any kind of "historical" or even anecdotal accuracy. You have been warned; I hope you have enjoyed the ride.

I have always had the unshakable belief that every single human being has some knowledge of important elements of beauty and substance, whether everybody else knows them or not, and the appropriate introduction of those items of intellectual power into the public discourse has been the unswerving thrust of my work, whatever form it took, all my life.

Chronology of the Life of Bess Lomax Hawes

1867	Father, John Avery Lomax, born on September 23 at Goodman, Mississippi
1880	Mother, Bess Bauman Brown, born on October 23 at Austin, Texas
1904	Marriage of John Lomax and Bess Brown on June 9 at Austin, Texas
1905	Sister Shirley Lomax born on August 7 at Austin, Texas
1907	Brother John Avery Lomax Jr. born on June 14 at Austin, Texas
1915	Brother Alan James Lomax born on January 31 at Austin, Texas
1921	Bess Brown Lomax Jr. [Bess Lomax Hawes] born on January 21 at Austin, Texas
1925	Lomax family relocates to Dallas, Texas
1931	Death of mother, Bess Bauman Brown Lomax, on May 8 at Dallas, Texas
1934	Marriage of John A. Lomax to Ruby Rochelle Terrill on July 21 at Commerce, Texas
1935–36	Student at the University of Texas, Austin, Texas
1936	Lomax family relocates to Washington, D.C.
1938	Travel in Europe, February–September
1938–41	Student at Bryn Mawr College, Bryn Mawr, Pennsylvania
1943	Marriage to Baldwin (Butch) Hawes on January 30 at New York City
1946	Daughter Corey born on January 21 at New York City
1947	Daughter Naomi born on September 1 at Boston, Massachusetts
1948	Death of father, John A. Lomax, on January 26 at Greenville, Mississippi
1948	Son Nicholas born on August 24 at Brookline, Massachusetts
1951	Hawes family relocates to California in March
1961	Death of stepmother, Ruby Terrill Lomax, on December 28 at Houston, Texas
1970	Obtains Master of Arts degree in folklore from University of California at Berkeley
1971	Death of husband Baldwin (Butch) Hawes on December 21 at Santa Monica, California
1974	Death of brother John Lomax Jr. on December 12 at Houston, Texas
1992	Retires from National Endowment for the Arts
1995	Relocates to California
1996	Death of sister Shirley Lomax Mansell Duggan on September 3 at Tulsa, Oklahoma
2002	Death of brother Alan Lomax on July 19 at Safety Harbor, Florida
2007	Relocates to Oregon

Index

Music in American Life

Tito Puente and the Making of Latin Music   *Steven Loza*

Juilliard: A History   *Andrea Olmstead*

Understanding Charles Seeger, Pioneer in American Musicology   *Edited by*
  Bell Yung and Helen Rees

Mountains of Music: West Virginia Traditional Music from *Goldenseal*   *Edited by*
  John Lilly

Alice Tully: An Intimate Portrait   *Albert Fuller*

A Blues Life   *Henry Townsend, as told to Bill Greensmith*

Long Steel Rail: The Railroad in American Folksong (2d ed.)   *Norm Cohen*

The Golden Age of Gospel   *Text by Horace Clarence Boyer; photography by*
  Lloyd Yearwood

Aaron Copland: The Life and Work of an Uncommon Man   *Howard Pollack*

Louis Moreau Gottschalk   *S. Frederick Starr*

Race, Rock, and Elvis   *Michael T. Bertrand*

Theremin: Ether Music and Espionage   *Albert Glinsky*

Poetry and Violence: The Ballad Tradition of Mexico's Costa Chica
  John H. McDowell

The Bill Monroe Reader   *Edited by Tom Ewing*

Music in Lubavitcher Life   *Ellen Koskoff*

Zarzuela: Spanish Operetta, American Stage   *Janet L. Sturman*

Bluegrass Odyssey: A Documentary in Pictures and Words, 1966–86
  Carl Fleischhauer and Neil V. Rosenberg

That Old-Time Rock & Roll: A Chronicle of an Era, 1954–63   *Richard Aquila*

Labor's Troubadour   *Joe Glazer*

American Opera   *Elise K. Kirk*

Don't Get above Your Raisin': Country Music and the Southern Working Class
  Bill C. Malone

John Alden Carpenter: A Chicago Composer   *Howard Pollack*

Heartbeat of the People: Music and Dance of the Northern Pow-wow
  Tara Browner

My Lord, What a Morning: An Autobiography   *Marian Anderson*

Marian Anderson: A Singer's Journey   *Allan Keiler*

Charles Ives Remembered: An Oral History   *Vivian Perlis*

Henry Cowell, Bohemian   *Michael Hicks*

Rap Music and Street Consciousness   *Cheryl L. Keyes*

Louis Prima   *Garry Boulard*

Marian McPartland's Jazz World: All in Good Time   *Marian McPartland*

Robert Johnson: Lost and Found   *Barry Lee Pearson and Bill McCulloch*

Bound for America: Three British Composers   *Nicholas Temperley*

Lost Sounds: Blacks and the Birth of the Recording Industry, 1890–1919
  Tim Brooks

The University of Illinois Press
is a founding member of the
Association of American University Presses.

Composed in 10/13.5 Janson Text
with Electra display
by Barbara Evans
at the University of Illinois Press
Manufactured by Cushing-Malloy, Inc.

University of Illinois Press
1325 South Oak Street
Champaign, IL 61820-6903
www.press.uillinois.edu